Who Am I?

Who Am I?

A Spiritual Life

ROB GIESELMANN

RESOURCE *Publications* · Eugene, Oregon

WHO AM I?
A Spiritual Life

Copyright © 2025 Rob Gieselmann. All rights reserved. Except for brief quotations in critical publications or reviews, no part of this book may be reproduced in any manner without prior written permission from the publisher. Write: Permissions, Wipf and Stock Publishers, 199 W. 8th Ave., Suite 3, Eugene, OR 97401.

Resource Publications
An Imprint of Wipf and Stock Publishers
199 W. 8th Ave., Suite 3
Eugene, OR 97401

www.wipfandstock.com

PAPERBACK ISBN: 979-8-3852-4926-8
HARDCOVER ISBN: 979-8-3852-4927-5
EBOOK ISBN: 979-8-3852-4928-2
VERSION NUMBER 09/12/25

Scripture quotations are from New Revised Standard Version Bible, copyright © 1989 National Council of the Churches of Christ in the United States of America. Used by permission. All rights reserved worldwide.

For Paul and Reenie, with love and gratitude.

This is the nature of mature, mystical religion—simple and clear. We shave away as many religious assumptions and judgments as possible and re-ground religion on one lone assumption—a divine love that can only be experienced and not proved by rational logic.

—Richard Rohr[1]

1. Rohr, Richard, *The Tears of Things*, copyright by Center for Action and Contemplation, Inc., New York, NY, Convergent Books (Penguin/Random House), 2025, p. 143.

Contents

Timeline | ix
Preface | xi

One: Faith without Warning | 1
Two: God Lives | 4
Three: Who am I? | 5
Four: Surprised by Love | 7
Five: The Blind Man | 15
Six: Religion | 21
Seven: From Faith to Pharisee | 23
Eight: Who do you say that I am? | 31
Nine: From Pharisee to Faith From Blindness to Love | 34
Ten: Jacob Bests God | 38
Eleven: The Word of God | 43
Twelve: Holy Scripture | 48
Thirteen: Exploration | 51
Fourteen: I will Never Leave You | 55
Fifteen: The Rotation of Faith | 59
Sixteen: Possession | 61
Seventeen: Control | 63
Eighteen: The Prayer for Honesty | 67
Nineteen: Certainty: Providence | 69
Twenty: Guidance: Holy Spirit | 74
Twenty-One: Love | 76

Twenty-Two: The Sea Vista, I | 82
Twenty-Three: The Complexities | 86
Twenty-Four: Sincerity | 93
Twenty-Five: The Hardest Love | 95
Twenty-Six: The Sea Vista, II | 105
Twenty-Seven: The Blowing Snow | 108
Twenty-Eight: Worship the Lord...in spirit and in truth... | 111
Twenty-Nine: Sex and Sexuality | 118
Thirty: Shells | 124
Thirty-One: Behind the Veil | 127
Thirty-Two: Projections and God | 132
Thirty-Three: A Habit of Prayer | 137
Thirty-Four: God, Past Present Future | 141
Thirty-Five: Prayer | 143
Thirty-Six: What does the Lord Ordaineth? | 147
Thirty-Seven: ThanksGiving | 150
Thirty-Eight: Creation and Salvation | 153
Thirty-Nine: Who am I? | 157
Forty: Who are you, O God? | 160

Timeline

1931, 1933—Paul (Daddy) and Reenie (Mom) born

1954, 1956—Butch and Nancy born

1958—Rob Born, third of four children

1961—Pete born

1964—Move from Knoxville, TN to Vero Beach, FL, to live at the Sea Vista

1970—Christian Confirmation

1972—"Baptism in the Holy Spirit"

1977—Daddy (Paul) died

1978—Joined Maranatha

1979—Graduated college, began graduate school in Economics

1983—Quit Maranatha

1984—Completed graduate school in Economics (MS)

1987—Graduated law school (The University of Tennessee)

1987-1996—Practiced law in Knoxville, TN

1992—Married Laura

1994—Tate born

1996—1999—Seminary at University of the South

TIMELINE

1997—Tilly born

1999, 2000—Ordained deacon, then priest, serving in TN

2001 to 2005—Served as Rector, St. Paul's Parish, Chestertown, MD

2002, June—Laura died at home in Chestertown

2005 to 2010—Served as Rector, Christ Church, Sausalito, CA

2010 to 2015—Served as Rector, St. Stephen's Church, Tiburon/Belvedere, CA

2015 to 2017—Served as Rector, Church of the Ascension, Knoxville, TN

2018—Retired and walked Camino de Santiago

2018—Mom/Reenie died

2019—Served as Interim Rector, St. Thomas, Sun Valley, ID

2020—Continued retirement

2022—Served as Interim Rector, St. Stephen's Church, Tiburon/Belvedere, CA

Preface

I WROTE A THESIS for a degree in economics many years ago and submitted it to my three-professor team the same month I started law school. I naively thought that submitting it would be enough, that my professors would pass me without comment. However, my lead professor, David Whitten, happened to be an editor for Wall Street Review, the Saturday book review section of the Wall Street Journal. He knew *good* writing. He also knew *bad* writing. Mine was not exactly "bad," but it certainly was not "good."

Professor Whitten reviewed the first third of that original draft, bleeding liberally on each page to teach me how to improve my writing. Returning the draft, he noted that although my grammar was *adequate,* as in technically sound, my style was terrible. He suggested I purchase a copy of that old classic, *Elements of Style*, (Strunk and White), and concluded his note by suggesting that I (and these are his exact words) *"not submit my thesis again in substandard form."*

The thing about spiritual experience is this: most of us think that our first experience makes us experts, yet a singular experience leaves a person in substandard spiritual form. A neophyte, a beginner. Relationship with God is not a one-and-done event. Deeper connection usually means practice, years of growth, decades of development. *Refinement by fire,* the writer to the Hebrews calls it, and I have to wonder—don't you?—whether God actually builds the refiner's fire or let's life build it? Regardless, the question for each of us is whether or not we will choose to engage and thereby go deeper. Engagement means both holding on and letting go.

I am told that letting go is the first step to spiritual experiences in each of the major religions. To find the Divine, the Holy, to experience the purest of loves. Letting go, trusting beyond yourself, is the challenge wall. However, letting go suggests there is something being held onto.

Jacob (later, "Israel") would not let go of God until he pinned God down. He started the fight, and by-God he was going to finish it. He held on before he finally let go.

Which, of course, begs the question as each of us moves through life: when do we fight and when do we let go? How long do you hold on? And what is it you hold on to? If letting go is the first step, why not just let go and be done with it? Jacob spent decades before letting go.

At the most impossible moments of my journey of faith, when I had tried my hardest, held on as long as I could, yet finally let go, the only thing I was left with was my faith—and not even that. Not *my* faith, but God's. Or, not faith at all, all I was left with was God and God alone.

This same God-alone is the One who sustained me throughout both struggle and release, over and over and over again.

The book you are holding presents as a memoir, even a spiritual memoir. Yet, I would rather call it a story about God. And grace. And the incomparable and inexhaustible love of God. My hope is that you, as reader, will find these chapters helpful as you consider and interpret your own story.

By the way, I spent that first Christmas break from law school revising and finishing the thesis, top to bottom. Because, as my grandmother said, "*You should always finish what you started.*"

One

Faith without Warning

FAITH[1] FOUND ME WITHOUT warning. I did not seek faith. To the extent I'd heard of something called, *faith*, I did not know what it might be or offer. I am still not sure I know—not really—although I am fairly sure of this: faith barely touches the cerebral activity most people think of when they consider faith. Faith is not the intellectualizing or understanding of God or life or the universe, at least in the way religion typically treats it.

For me, faith came uninvited when I knelt beside my mom, beside her bed, on teenage knees, my broken soul clothed in the teenage angst of cut-off jeans and a dirty t-shirt. I prayed to receive the Holy Spirit in that charismatic fashion that my mom urged on me. I spoke in gibberish tongues[2] as she guided.

> 1. What is faith? People typically think of faith as "belief", meaning brainpower, or perhaps an intentional response to deity, who we call, "God". When I use the term, "faith", I intend for it to mean relationship, just like any other relationship. A person leans into relationship, lets it grow and evolve, and expects it to be imperfect.
>
> 2. Tongues as a spiritual exercise or experience refer to the outpouring of the Holy Spirit, as at Pentecost—Acts, chapter 2—and in the modern experience, as expressed by the Pentecostal movement of the twentieth century. That movement spilled into mainline denominations, such as the Roman Catholic and Episcopal Churches, dubbed the "Charismatic Movement." "Tongues" becomes a type of prayer—for the most part—that an individual expresses

And for perhaps the first time in my life, I felt loved, completely loved, and completely accepted.

"In the beginning was the Word, and the Word was with God, and the Word was God. He[3] was in the beginning with God," (Jn. 1:1–2), and somehow and improbably Word as Spirit exploded in

---

when that person is unsure of how or for what to pray—in theory, letting the Holy Spirit pray through him or her. The sound and experience of speaking in tongues is that of a child pretending to speak in a foreign language. I offer no judgment as to whether tongues are truly an expression of the Divine, but would like to observe that the practice of tongues is similar to that of centering prayer, in both cases resulting in the removal of thought processes, brain power, in the prayer experience, allowing the deeper parts of a human being to become more open to God.

3. I use various pronouns for God throughout, including masculine, feminine and plural, in the recognition that God is, after all, genderless, and both singular and plural.

my chest. I realized imperceptibly that I, too, was with God at the beginning. From the beginning. That there was no beginning, is no middle nor end.

I quit Mom's bedside to return upstairs to my own room, where I continued to speak in a strange language as an open doorway into a different world. I received something that, unbeknownst to me then, I would retain in one form or another the rest of my life: A place. To go. When my world would become chaotic. When I would not only feel—but be—attacked or betrayed. When I would lose and feel loss. Broken hearted. And even when I would win.

A place. To go. Inside. With words as pathway. With silence as throughway. Always deep within.

Two

God Lives

"God lives, right here." Pounding our chests in church, the preacher as mantra had us repeat the words over and over again. "God lives, right here. Right here, God lives."

As in, "God is good. All the time. All the time. God is good."

As in, "In the beginning was the Word." The Word was with God. The Word that is God was and is and is to come. God. And each morning, still in love, held in love, I am invited to return to the moment of my creation.

A place. To go. And each morning afresh, anew, I return.

Three

Who am I?

"Who are you, O God?" St. Francis is reported to have asked daily. And, "Who am *I*?"

Who am I? I am a priest, although perhaps not a very good one. I do not live as others think I should live. I am not particularly religious[1], and I am not particularly fond of people who are. Or, rather, I am not fond of people being religious for the sake of religion. Because, you see, I do not like religion existing for its own sake. Nor order for the sake of order. Nor hierarchy for the sake of hierarchy. Nor tall hats with short souls.

I am, however, a believer. I believe in hope. I believe in Jesus. I also believe in Jesus as the Christ, although I tend to believe more in Jesus, the un-deified human being full of God and grace, a person I can relate to more than the deified Christ. But I also believe in a God who lives both in heaven and inside of me. Eternity positioned against terminus. And I believe most of all in love. A love like wind that blows from the west, pushes through, whirls about

---

1. When I write of being religious or of religion, I mean the institutionalization of the experience of God, either by religious structures and hierarchy, or the practice of religion through liturgy. Both the structures and liturgy are intended to serve the relationship one or a group has with/to the Divine, and not become the end in themselves.

me, and then continues eastward. Never stays, yet never leaves. Never sharp, yet never dull.

A fire. A candle. A light. A darkness.

Who am I? I am a friend. A lover. A father and a mother.

A seeker, and now that I am sixty-four, I am just about settled.

A reader and a writer, a poet and an artist. I abide midway between my right brain and left.

An eco-ologist. Though like being priest, I am not particularly good at this, either. I just know that—I cannot "walk past the color purple in a field and not notice."[2]

I am an athlete. And a gardener.

And at least for today, I am both a priest and a human being, as I review my own internal spiritual life and struggles, and I am also a writer of the same. It is because I believe that I write, because I connect that I tell, and because I see in others hope that I share. About grace.

---

2. Walker, Alice, *The Color Purple*, London, Penguin Books (Reprint Edition), 2019.

Four

Surprised by Love

Just lost when I was saved!
Just felt the world go by!
Just girt me for the onset with eternity,
When breath blew back,
And on the other side
I heard recede the disappointed tide!

—Emily Dickenson

A. 1972: THE INVITATION

THE SUMMER BEFORE I turned fourteen, Mom took us on vacation. She had just divorced my dad and wanted to get away with just the four of us kids. We were teenagers, or mostly so, who each in our own way were poking the barely-warm ashes of our doused family fire.

Daddy was missing, though I did not miss him.

We were walking along the beach, the five of us, pushing sticks into crab holes and hoping to find sand dollars washed-up on shore. Who among us appreciated the burden my mother bore?

A now dissolved marriage from an alcoholic man, leaving her with dysfunctional mess to clean-up. How do you help four kids who don't know that they need help? Who don't realize that the world they've lived in their entire lives is wrong? That up should be up, and not down, as it had been during most of our lives?

How do you save your kids when you don't know how to save yourself?

But Mom had recently found religion, or should I say? Religion found her. She experienced what is known euphemistically as the "Baptism in the Holy Spirit". The Charismatic Movement was a pentecostal extension of the late sixties' Jesus Movement that had worked its way into mainline churches, including our Episcopal Church. Although she had, she later told me, answered an evangelical altar call when she was a teenager, she had never lived the life. This time made all the difference. She became revitalized, once dead and now alive. Finding additional support through Al Anon, Mom began to understand that she was not responsible for my father's emotional alienation.

She now wanted to fix our broken family, she also wanted to honor her newfound faith. Her faith—depending heavily on a literal interpretation of the Bible—would eventually lead her back to my father. She read Jesus' words against divorce, declaring it to be permissible only in cases of adultery. Jesus spoke the admonition as a counter to the hypocrites, religious leaders who treated women dismissively as property. Unfortunately for me, Mom's literal reading of Jesus' words would be to my detriment, as I was happiest during the time they were divorced. With my father's eventual return came both alcohol and chaos. But, I am getting ahead of myself.

So there we were, meandering along the shore while the tide of waves washed at our feet as solace to the shore, when Mom offered her oyster's pearl. "If any of you would like to be baptized in the Holy Spirit, let me know."

Holy Spirit. I didn't know the Holy Spirit before now. I didn't know there *was* a Holy Spirit, though I'd heard vague references to "Holy Ghost" in church and from snippets I'd read in my King James Bible. Ghost, as though God might be *dead*.

That short offering was all Mom gave, nothing more, just simple invitation.

B. THE ANSWER

I suppose I wanted to please Mom. No, that was not it. Or was it? I was the *good* child, after all, the role I played in our family drama. What better way to be *good* than to do what your mother suggests as being *good*? Still, that was not it. I've learned over the years to distinguish between that which compels me psychologically from inside myself and that which guides me from outside myself. The pull I felt over the coming weeks was from outside, wholly extrinsic to me, and not from my complex though immature psychology. I was being pulled into a vortex, and I had no choice, none at all.

Two weeks later with just the two of us alone in the house, I trepidatiously approached Mom. "I want to receive the Holy Spirit," I stammered. Or whatever it was you meant. Whatever that is. Here I am.

C. THE NATURE OF RESPONSE

Here I am, like Isaiah the prophet. Here I am, use me. Only Isaiah was an iconoclast, a hero of heroes, and I was a frightened boy, more child than man. My response—if you can call it that—was more like Mary's, Jesus' mother's: "[L]et be with me" as you have said. (Lk. 1:38) I wonder. What if Mary had refused? Said, "No?" Could I have said, "No?" Or did my life change because I said, "Yes?" Even the simple answer of, "Yes," smacks of exchange. An offer and acceptance, a contract. As though I acted in such a way that I might receive, or that God made an offer requiring a response on my part. Paint by numbers, grace-by-works, and you get a little help, but such would still be a do-it-yourself faith, which may be no faith at all. As one writer put it, "We love because he first loved us." (1 Jn. 4:19) Neither love nor "yes" originate from within me.

Faith isn't some Texas two-step. It isn't two-dimensional: 1. God calls. 2. I respond. Rather, the exchange between the human soul and the Divine is mystical, swirling about, impossible to dissect and equally impossible to understand. "I believe," only the very word itself, "believe," is impotent, or at least imprecise. I give myself to? I donate myself to? I lean into? I am pulled into? I am drawn, inexorably drawn, like an undertow that pulls me, ever against my will, out to a churning sea?

For I did not "accept Jesus as my savior"; I did not give my life to God; I neither understood nor appreciated the Doctrine of the Trinity, the Incarnation, the Resurrection or the flow and gift of the Holy Spirit, as at Pentecost; I did not consider Jesus to be the "way, the truth and the life." (Jn. 14:6) I did not beg forgiveness for my sins. I did not get circumcised in order to please God. It never occurred that there might be hoops one must jump through in order to receive grace. I wasn't even looking for it, this thing called grace. I made no promises. To God. To anyone.

Jesus said children have a much easier time grasping God—*believing*—not because they do something, but because they do nothing. They erect no walls to faith, engage no mental blockages, concoct no scientific exceptions, complain of experiential failings. They simply are—simply human—simply children. Simply and earnestly available. "Let the little children come to me, and do not stop them; for it is to such as these that the kingdom of heaven belongs." (Mt. 19:14)

And what exactly did I do? The question is red herring, for I did nothing.

Why is it, then, that religion so often becomes a wall that blocks people out, away from grace?

D. THE EVENT

That night, Jesus, the Holy Spirit, the Divine, the Maker of the Universe, the Holiest of Holy Ones, El Shaddai, the force behind the shimmering veil captured me, and has held onto me ever since. Even when I might have let go. Even when I have let go.

I knelt down next to Mom at her bedside. She laid a hand on my shoulder, or perhaps it was my head, and she prayed for me. To receive the Holy Spirit. I followed her lead, and mimicked the gibberish "tongues" I heard her utter.

The words, the volume, the tenor of the gibberish is irrelevant. It was irrelevant then, just as it is now. What is relevant is this: in the exercise of yielding, of exercising the faith-step required to open my mouth, out spilled this exotic, childlike language, halting at first, then flowing with relief, as though the words had been pent-up within me from birth. Flowing with both vulnerability and grace. Tongues, and whether or not you believe in that sort of thing, something happened. To me. And I have never been the same.

This event was the most extraordinary—though perhaps it should be described as the smallest—thing. God entered the tiniest, most concealed dark corner within me, took up residence, and lit a match. My chest exploded as though with TNT, and I knew then, in that one instant, this one inexorable truth, that I am accepted. Just as I am. Without one plea.

E. THE NATURE OF THE EVENT (OR, SALVATION, WHATEVER THAT WORD MEANS)

It would be years before I could describe it in this more pastoral way, but *salvation* is, at the least, the realization of acceptance. That you are accepted. By God. In the Universe. As you are. Like I said, without one plea.

So many people spend lifetimes feeling as though they live outside on a street curb. Are not, and never have been, invited to join the club. Estranged, homeless, or just plain unloveable. Then along comes this unexpected, uninvited breeze called hope that exhales into the tiniest of crevasses. And whispers, you are as you are, you are who you are, and I love you exactly that way.

"Salvation" is a baggage word, one I have come to detest. As in, "Are you saved?" (*Why no, and how unattractive of you to remind me.*) As a religious term, it is linked inviolably to hell (saved from) and heaven (saved for). The word has become a line drawn in the sand. It is a way for one person to say to another, "I am in, and you, therefore, are out." Only the saved go to heaven (whatever or wherever "heaven" is).

Saved, not for heaven or hell, but for a meaningful existence here and now, on this earth. Kingdom of God to earth.

Christian Scriptures—the Bible—suggest at least four ways a person might be "saved", not just one as many Christian sects claim. "Sell your possessions," Jesus told the rich man. "Believe," Paul told the Romans. "Be baptized," Peter told his followers. Do good works, James told his readers. Doubtless there are thousands additional ways to life. Why limit God?

I didn't do any one or all of these things, yet I knew I was *saved* in that moment, not from hell, but in some other sense, hell and heaven having nothing to do with the *all* of the event. I was *saved* from—if you will—a meaningless existence. To live. A full life. Here and now. And, to be accepted, without one plea.

If you insist upon a method to be saved, then employ a method. Only, I ask that you do not limit God when it comes to others. Do not box God in. Divine Mystery responds most often by invitation, regardless of the form of invitation, and seldom to demand. Appears in any myriad of ways. In silence or in music. While gardening or cooking, even cleaning. And, of course, through nature. God in creation, walking through the Garden.

F. POSTSCRIPT THOUGHTS

Just this morning I experienced the same Divine love I felt fifty years ago, this time while snowshoeing with my dogs as we clambered up the side of a small mountain. Once on top, I looked out at the expanse of valleys and mountains before me, mountains upon mountains layered as lines of poetry, and what could I do, but breathe, breathe, and breathe?

I think often of Cornelius, in the Book of Acts, the patron saint of unorthodoxy. He defied both Christian method and Christian convention. The Holy Spirit came to him *before* he acknowledged Jesus to be Savior, before he was baptized, before he confessed anything verbally or made promises he could not keep. I claim Cornelius as my personal saint, for the Spirit of God came to me by her own volition, made my soul her bed and my heart her pillow.

I wonder where else the Divine has appeared unbidden, even unnoticed? I have one friend who experiences God most when he studies *about* God—brain to heart, somehow, and he becomes ever so animated! Other friends are poets, you can read grace between their lines. How is that possible? I think of Eric Liddell, who in the movie *Chariots of Fire* exclaimed, "When I run, I feel his pleasure."[1] I feel his pleasure when I paint. And when my bare hands dig in black dirt. For there, hands on earth, you can feel the heartbeat of God.

Why do we suppose God fails to show-up anywhere and everywhere there is a human being on this planet? Oh, my, of course that must be the case, that God shows-up always and everywhere, if indeed "God so love[s] the world . . ."

---

1. *Chariots of Fire*, directed by Hugh Hudson (1981; Burbank, CA: Warner Bros., 2000), DVD.

And God does so love the world, and the people it contains. And cares about their pain.

I was in pain, you see. At fourteen, when I knelt beside my mother. Perhaps the *good* child, but ever the lost child. I so craved the love of someone, anyone, but especially my father, though it would be years and maybe a lifetime before I realized how incapable he was of giving me that love. Still, there, on my knees, vulnerable in the way a teenage boy is not supposed to be vulnerable, love entered my chest. Held me tight, and even now, after all these years, still holds me ever tight.

Five

The Blind Man

As [Jesus] walked along, he saw a man blind from birth. His disciples asked him, "Rabbi, who sinned, this man or his parents, that he was born blind?" Jesus answered, "Neither this man nor his parents sinned; he was born blind so that God's works might be revealed in him. We must work the works of him who sent me while it is day; night is coming when no one can work. As long as I am in the world, I am the light of the world." When he had said this, he spat on the ground and made mud with the saliva and spread the mud on the man's eyes, saying to him, "Go, wash in the pool of Siloam" (which means Sent). Then he went and washed and came back able to see. The neighbors and those who had seen him before as a beggar began to ask, "Is this not the man who used to sit and beg?" Some were saying, "It is he." Others were saying, "No, but it is someone like him." He kept saying, "I am the man." But they kept asking him, "Then how were your eyes opened?" He answered, "The man called Jesus made mud, spread it on my eyes, and said to me, 'Go to Siloam and wash.' Then I went and washed and received my sight." They said to him, "Where is he?" He said, "I do not know."

WHO AM I?

They brought to the Pharisees the man who had formerly been blind. Now it was a sabbath day when Jesus made the mud and opened his eyes. Then the Pharisees also began to ask him how he had received his sight. He said to them, "He put mud on my eyes. Then I washed, and now I see." Some of the Pharisees said, "This man is not from God, for he does not observe the sabbath." But others said, "How can a man who is a sinner perform such signs?" And they were divided. So they said again to the blind man, "What do you say about him? It was your eyes he opened." He said, "He is a prophet."

The [religious leaders] did not believe that he had been blind and had received his sight until they called the parents of the man who had received his sight and asked them, "Is this your son, who you say was born blind? How then does he now see?" His parents answered, "We know that this is our son, and that he was born blind; but we do not know how it is that now he sees, nor do we know who opened his eyes. Ask him; he is of age. He will speak for himself." His parents said this because they were afraid of the Jews; for the Jews had already agreed that anyone who confessed Jesus to

---

1. The Healing of the Blind Man (and the Raising of Lazarus, cropped), artist unknown, exhibited at The Cloisters, New York City, public domain.

be the Messiah would be put out of the synagogue. Therefore his parents said, "He is of age; ask him."

So for the second time they called the man who had been blind, and they said to him, "Give glory to God! We know that this man is a sinner." He answered, "I do not know whether he is a sinner. One thing I do know, that though I was blind, now I see." They said to him, "What did he do to you? How did he open your eyes?" He answered them, "I have told you already, and you would not listen. Why do you want to hear it again? Do you also want to become his disciples?" Then they reviled him, saying, "You are his disciple, but we are disciples of Moses. We know that God has spoken to Moses, but as for this man, we do not know where he comes from." The man answered, "Here is an astonishing thing! You do not know where he comes from, and yet he opened my eyes. We know that God does not listen to sinners, but he does listen to one who worships him and obeys his will. Never since the world began has it been heard that anyone opened the eyes of a person born blind. If this man were not from God, he could do nothing." They answered him, "You were born entirely in sins, and are you trying to teach us?" And they drove him out.

Jesus heard that they had driven him out, and when he found him, he said, "Do you believe in the Son of Man?" He answered, "And who is he, sir? Tell me, so that I may believe in him." Jesus said to him, "You have seen him, and the one speaking with you is he." He said, "Lord, I believe." And he worshiped him. Jesus said, "I came into this world for judgment so that those who do not see may see, and those who do see may become blind." Some of the Pharisees near him heard this and said to him, "Surely we are not blind, are we?" Jesus said to them, "If you were blind, you would not have sin. But now that you say, 'We see,' your sin remains. John, Chapter 9 (NRSV)

I WONDER WHETHER THE man who was born blind—the man to whom Jesus gave sight—had ever experienced an ounce of acceptance prior to his encounter with Jesus? Had *anybody* ascribed dignity to this creation of God? His parents? Religious devotees? Teachers?

WHO AM I?

Even Jesus' disciples disdain the man. Though largely undefined by John in his Gospel, these men set the scene by asking Jesus, "Who sinned for this man to have been born blind?"

Oh. My. Gosh. The disciples have learnt nothing. Here we are, halfway through the Gospel story, and they have learnt nothing.

Jesus immediately dispels a lifelong and societal myth: *No one sinned.*

"How this can be?" the disciples wonder. They, *you see*, are blind. The Jewish religious leaders, too, are blind, for neither do they understand. Only two people in this story *see*, only two people know that the man has done nothing to deserve his curse: the man himself, plus Jesus.

"I am the light of the World."

This man, blind from birth, only Jesus spits into mud, pastes the mud onto the man's eyes, and sends the man to wash in the very pool that means, *sent*, Siloam, and, I wonder, don't you? As friends lead him along the pathway to the Pool of Sent, *what typhoon of thoughts swirl about in this man's chaotic brain?* Does he doubt? Does he believe? Does he both doubt and believe? Maybe he *wonders*.

Sent and led in wonder, along the same pathways he had stumbled so blindly along in the past, never having seen the cobbled surface, never having noticed the chipmunks darting from stump to tree, is he apprehending this time with hope? Or anxiety? Perhaps anticipation? I can practically feel the sacred chakra in the man's belly yawing as he walks the fifteen minutes to wash. Mud waxes across his eyelids, you are earth and to earth you shall return, you are dust and to dust you shall return.

Spit. Typically derisive, used to curse, so Jesus spits into mud derisively. He *hates* how this man has been treated. The man had absorbed hate from others like a sponge his entire life. "Who sinned for this man to have been born blind?" Jesus cringes at his disciples' words, and those of the man's parents. Even they refuse his defense. "Ask him yourself," they retort. "Who sinned, this man or his parents?" Ask him yourself, for it certainly wasn't us. We did nothing wrong, they defend themselves at his expense, placing their son as their buffer between themselves and the religious leaders.

The sins of the parents rest heavily on the children. On this man's head. Do they love him? Or is he their scourge? His blindness is a banner telling everyone about his parents: They, too, are bad, or they would not have borne a blind son. Ask him yourself.

We must get to the bottom of this. And, so must the Jewish leaders. Who sinned? If not this man. Jesus alone feels no urgency to get to the bottom of this, certainly not with the man. No one sinned. Words that dispel the pop-philosophy of their day. Worse, and in the face of religious convention, Jesus breaks the law by healing. The man. On the Sabbath, when work is proscribed by religion. Heals this *sinner* whom even God has abandoned. Born that way, born in sin. They are sure of it.

Somebody sinned. Who was it? Where is the man? Find him, so we can ask him.

Only it is not this man who has sinned. Not this blind man. These men, these so-called leaders, are blind. They are blind to the invitation of Sabbath and see it only as rejection. Don't you see? Sabbath, though, is a *move into,* not a *refrain from.* Slow down. Enter into the realm of God. The flow of spirit. Breathe in, breathe out. Breathe in, breathe out. Siloam, Sent. Water flows from fresh springs into the pool, and out of the pool, and down across the hillside. The fresh flow of creation, and all a person needs to do to honor Sabbath is simple: flow with grace by breath. And rest.

The blind man on Sabbath is found walking into *his* Sabbath. "All I know is that I was blind, but now I see."

You know, looking back on my experience of the Holy Spirit at that naive but sweet age of fourteen—and it was an experience of the Holy Spirit—I consider many things. It is true. That August night became a dateline I crossed in my life from some lost era into an Alice in Wonderland time I'd not yet known—complete love, complete acceptance, all by some external that expressed itself internally to me. God lives, right here. I, too, washed blindness away in the Pool of Sent.

Perhaps I should build a shrine to my experience. To proclaim that because God exploded into my world in such and such a way, that is the experience everybody should have. "You must receive the Holy Spirit by laying on of hands." Only, not all people need to wash in the Pool to receive their sight, physical or otherwise. Enshrining experience by religious stricture blinds and binds. Oh, the Pharisees, they enshrined a faith that excluded rather than included possibility. Restricted Spirit rather than facilitated. Theirs became the *only* way.

Jesus, the *Way*. Yet Jesus *saw* faith as Gumby-like: malleable, bendable, shapeable, so different for each person. The blind man needed to walk to Siloam. The lame man needed friends to lower him into the living room through a hole in the roof. The woman with the hemorrhage needed to touch Jesus' cloak. And I needed to kneel at the bed beside my mother.

Faith finds us as we are and where we are, for each in their unique way. God finds us as we are and where we are, for each in their unique way. I once was lost, but now am found—only I was never lost. Not really. And neither are you.

Six

Religion

IN HIS BOOK, *THE Meaning of Happiness*, Alan Watts compares religious experience to artistic or musical inspiration. The spiritual experience occurs when the soul feels a profound happiness in the *whole of life*. A person feels united to the power behind the universe and thus first lives a life accordingly and second translates the feeling into thoughts and words. In turn, those who have not experienced the feeling will take what they perceive from that first person and formulate religion, both theological and moral.[1]

Watts later writes of *Tao* and *Nirvana*, two Buddhist experiences, as the names for the experiences and not the experiences themselves, lamenting that people seem so concerned with the names of the experiences that they forget the experience.[2]

Christianity was first an experience, starting of course with Abraham's encounter of God as One, and continuing through the early disciples' hands-on experience with both Jesus as the Christ and the Holy Spirit at Pentecost. Theology is the set of words used to describe the experience, and religion is the structured practice or reenactment of the experience. It becomes terribly easy to

---

1. Watts, Alan W., *The Meaning of Happiness*, Stanford, CA, James Ladd Delking (copyright 1940, second ed.), p. 41.
2. Watts, p. 165.

confuse the words—theology and religion—for the experience itself. The experience is primary and the descriptors are secondary. The descriptors are useful so long as they facilitate primary experience. When they become an end to themselves, they are not only unhelpful, they are dangerous.

Seven

From Faith to Pharisee

Jesus didn't die for us so we could continue treating people the way people treated him.

—Anonymous Facebook post, 2023

A. INTRODUCTION: THE INITIAL MOVEMENT

I don't know how it happens. It just happens. The movement away from *faith* to Pharisee.[1] When a guileless soul so happy to be alive, accepted and loved, morphs into someone unrecognizable, into a person who confuses rules for faith, a rulebook for life-giving Scripture.

One day, someone told me, "Jesus is either Lord of all, or he's not Lord at all." And I believed it. I tried to make Jesus or God or

---

1. "Pharisees" were Jewish religious leaders during the second Temple time (the time of Jesus and of the Roman occupation of the "promised land"). Pharisees believed in strict observance of the law (Torah) and the writings of the prophets. The term as used in Christian scriptures often indicates a person—essentially a caricature of a person—who would impose impossible religious requirements on others while hypocritically ignoring his own religious or moral failures.

Spirit or Father or Mother or Mystery or Creator or Regenerator into someone from whom I needed to earn the love I'd already received, the acceptance I'd already enjoyed. The love I still needed, the acceptance I still craved. How can one who has received a shot of grace so undeservedly mistake faith as something to be earned? Not that my confusion happened consciously, not that I made some decision, and not that it was any more than subtle erosion. Pharisaism is typically a building constructed slowly, day by day, month by month, brick by bloody brick.

My father—Daddy—died when I was eighteen, the August following my freshman year in college. I'd gone to work at Yellowstone National Park in a restaurant, and he died. I felt both relief and the void of grief.

From that point forward, I was on my own, financially and otherwise. Sailing a windless ocean, floating in a rudderless boat.

Of course Mom was still alive, but she was forging her own way, financially and otherwise, leaving me to become an adult by subtle alienation; I was now on my own.

In the world of sibling order, third of four, I am considered the lost child. I felt lost. So the following year, when a campus ministry—Maranatha, a Greek New Testament word which means "Come, Lord Jesus"—came to town, I joined. "Jesus is either Lord of all or not Lord at all." I heard. Either/or, black/white, vocabulary contrasts used by the fundamentalist to define life. You're either in or out. There is our way and there is the wrong way.

I craved clarity and these people offered it.[2] They told me what I needed to believe. And, they were suspicious of any previous religious experience, mostly because they had not engineered it.

B. RE-BAPTISM

They also told me I needed to be baptized a second time. The first time didn't take, they warned.

I had been baptized as a baby in the Episcopal Church. Someone—probably my godparents—gave me a prayer book, the Episcopal Book of Common Prayer, 1929 ed.[3] (as Modified by the 1979 Book of Common Prayer, "BCP"). Originally organized by Thomas Cromwell in the 1500s, the prayer book is exquisitely rich with phrases such as, "to know you is eternal life", and, "to serve you is perfect freedom"; and, "in whom we live and move and have our being." BCP, pp. 99–100.

The Episcopal Church—though rife with people of faith, abundant with people who care, teeming with people of grace, populated by people who pray and meditate, serve and love—was, these new "friends" told me, compromised. And of course they

---

2. I am telling this story because, as my friend, Joe Jennings, points out, each person's unique psychological constitution affects his or her spirituality—how they connect with God.

3. Throughout this book, I will refer to the 1979 edition of The Book of Common Prayer as, "BCP", with page number. *The Book of Common Prayer.* New York: Church Publishing, 1979.

were right, the Episcopal Church is compromised. As it turns out, every human life is compromised, were we to be honest about it, but at nineteen, I believed their lie. "Jesus is either Lord of all, or he isn't Lord at all." You aren't a true Christian unless and until you've given it all.

As though anyone can give it all. *Real* Christians, it turns out, are ordinary people who struggle, who work at this phenomenon called faith, but never quite manage to do it right. Incomplete lovers who see faith gilded by doubt, or is it perhaps doubt gilded by faith?

You must be baptized again. "You were a baby," they told me. "As a baby, you did not have the requisite capacity to believe. Baptism requires belief—yours, not someone else's." As though believing is mental ascent and not a belonging.

So I was baptized that second time in a bathtub with a crowd of other college students—"believers"—squeezed into that tiny bathroom, watching, praying and prophesying. I am not mocking these believers, we were neophytes, all of us. They, like I, were struggling to make sense of their worlds. Each of us had been drawn to fundamentalism for the clarity it offered, our young adult lives having felt the first shifts of life's tectonic plates.

C. THE NATURE OF CHRISTIAN FUNDAMENTALISM AND SCRIPTURE

In Maranatha, we claimed to believe, but we believed in a love that responded to behavior, to some version of perfection. Ours was a Pharisaic theology, as some—maybe most—Christian theologies are, at their roots. You must believe enough, do enough, be good enough.

"Believing" itself becomes a work. Something you do rather than something you lean into. I would now say that faith is anything but static. It is dynamic, a relationship and not a condition. Like all good long-lasting relationship, it includes the element of struggle. Why, even the Apostle Paul wrote about his struggles in and with faith.

This type of dynamic faith relationship is described repeatedly through the narrative of Scripture. The Bible is a compendium of peoples' experiences of God, stories revealing failure as much as success, struggle as much as hope. There is Jacob, who wrestled with God, Sarah who laughed at God, David who loved God dearly yet lied to God, Abraham who was God's friend yet imagined God wanted him to kill his own son, and of course there is Peter who—when it counted the most—denied Jesus. The Bible is an abstract of imperfect lives, interpreted best when the reader considers the times in which the characters lived, the ways in which the writers shared, and the interaction, interdiction and interloping of God woven throughout.

In Maranatha, as similar to many Christian sects, we treated the Bible literally, as the literal Word of God. I have since realized that taking Scripture as the literal Word of God is both impossible and idolatrous. Further, treating Scripture as science, history, philosophy or even religious doctrine traps God within its pages like a cat in a cage. God needs to be freed from the words, not bound by them. Only when God is freed can the pages becomes scriptural in nature. Only when God emerges from between the words do we connect. From the white page between the words.

Paul wrote that, by grace, all things are lawful. Not necessarily expedient, but lawful. The broad land within which to live is that fenced by love. Responding to and acting in love *is* Scripture, living Scripture, and Scripture is Word only when bounded by love.

Or freed by love.

D. MY FAILURE (AND SUCCESS) AT FUNDAMENTALISM

So there I was, baptized a second time and spending the next five years, not to mention time after that—the hangover time—thinking and living as though grace was tagged like Minnie Pearl's hat with a purchase price. Only I could not, at the end of the day, pay the price that kind of grace required. I was a young man broke, without currency, much like the prodigal son. I finally realized that

I could not be not good enough, despite being the "good child." I failed miserably at Pharisaism.

Let me start by observing how each person's faith hinges on that person's psychological makeup and challenges, not just life's challenges. The same was and is true of me, much of where I have ended-up has hinged on my emotional and psychological challenges. In this instance, regarding my own faith and in those days, fundamentalism, I struggled with sex and sexuality. As most likely a bisexual, fundamentalist person with decidedly same-sex feelings, I tried hiding those impulses from both others and God, as though hiding like Adam from God in the garden were truly possible. Sadly, I'd fallen into the inevitable fundamentalist, Bible-literalist trap, that God would accept me only if I conformed to what I thought the Bible requires, that God loves only straight people. To be fair to the fundamentalist, I never would have admitted God loved me only if straight, and I would say to others, back in the day, that "God loves the sinner, but hates the sin." The rub is this: being gay, or bisexual, or even straight for that matter, is existential, a state of being, so deeply embedded in a person that being something other than whatever the person is becomes a lie. Living a lie, as they say, and they say it for a reason, I learned.

And so, I had become deeply dishonest, and I should add, lying not just to God and others, but to myself. You see, I've never been straight. God knew this about me when, at fourteen God contributed un-purchased and uncompromising love to me. God called me without "fixing" or altering my sexuality, God did not care then, just as God does not care now. But this part of God and God's love I did not appreciate, and certainly did not understand. I'm not even sure I had the language to speak of myself as bisexual in those days, and the fear of mixed feelings made me so deeply afraid of, God forbid, being gay. Pretend—pretense. I thought I could fool God, only—like they say, "You can run, but you cannot hide."

Living a so-called un-compromised life failed me. I just couldn't do it, at least not as they defined it, not with integrity. So what was I to do?

It was not until a handful of years later when I yelled at God, shook my fist, and declared, "Fine, if that's what you expect of me, then send me to hell." God and I, we had it out. Like Jacob and God.

But I am getting ahead of myself. Until then, from a year after my father died until I left Maranatha at twenty-five, I was a Pharisee, committed to living an impossible life.

It is a miserable existence, that of a Pharisee. To create your rule of life and impose it fiercely on yourself and judge others because they don't do the same. To tell others they are going to burn in an unquenchable fire. Suffer, suffer, suffer, you will surely suffer. Can you imagine? Telling yourself that? Only that's not the crux of it. The crux of it is judgment. Subconscious, sometimes, overt towards others. Right at the fore of the brain.

I am better than you. I am closer to God than you. God likes me more because I do it better than you. I am God's favorite. Perhaps God loves you, but accepts you fully only when you become like I am. Only when you think like I do. Only when you accept Jesus as your Lord and Savior the way I have. Standing at the altar and telling God how happy you are that you are not like that miserable sinner across the way. All the while feeling terribly alone and unaccepted, ever so deep within the soul.

The best response I've ever heard when someone asked her whether she was "saved" was that mentioned previously, by a friend's grandmother: "Why no, and how unattractive of you to remind me." She didn't allow herself to be sucked-in; she did not accept the premise of the question. She did not misconstrue salvation as being a heaven or hell event rather than a love relationship.

I made the mistake of accepting the premise of the question. Even when God had already "saved" me—that time in my life when heaven and hell did not matter, when nothing mattered other than figuring out how to live a life with less pain. God simply revealed to me a swept corner of love. For those years I was a Pharisee, I did the unthinkable. I rejected love thinking I could do it all by myself.

None of this was conscious, mind you, and even during those years, God showed-up. In little pieces. Here and there. Never left nor forsook me. That God of mine, so so so unfailingly loyal.

WHO AM I?

Yes, it is a terrible way to live, that life of a Pharisee. The Pharisee is miserable and won't be satisfied until everyone else is miserable with him. The Pharisee knows God to be harsh.

Eight

Who do you say that I am?

> *Jesus went on with his disciples to the villages of Caesarea Philippi, and on the way he asked his disciples, "Who do people say that I am?" And they answered him, "John the Baptist; and others, Elijah; and still others, one of the prophets." He asked them, "But who do you say that I am?" Peter answered him, "You are the Messiah." And he sternly ordered them not to tell anyone about him.* Mark 8:27–30 (NRSV)

JESUS ONCE TOLD A story about a man who, leaving on a trip, gave servants money to invest while he was away. Although both Matthew and Luke tell the story, I find Matthew's words to be most haunting.[1]

When the man returned from his trip, he called the servants to account. The first servant proudly told his master, "I earned five talents while you were gone." Excellent. The second likewise reported strong earnings from his investments. The third, however, the one who had been entrusted with the least, hid the money in the ground for safekeeping. Upon his master's return, he recovered the money and handed it back to him.

---

1. See Matthew 25, paraphrased by me throughout this chapter.

The prudent master interrogated the third man. "Why didn't you at least put the money in the bank to earn interest?"

To which the servant retorted, "I knew you to be a hard man, reaping where you do not sow, and taking what is not yours. So I hid the money for safekeeping until you returned."

This third man strikes a cord. How many people only know God to be harsh, are afraid of God? The philosophical foundation of the Pharisee is narrow rather than expansive, is based on an unhealthy fear that restricts him or herself, binds that person to the past. How we view God and how we read Scripture has everything with who God and Scripture are to each of us.

For me, regaining spiritual health ultimately hinged on my response to the question, "Who do I know God to be?" I certainly treated God as narrow in those days when I, too, lived as a Pharisee. I could neither see nor appreciate the expansive nature of God. I would never have said it, but God to me had become harsh.

There is a whole wonder of worlds out there in which to find God, yet I could find God only in the same miserable little place, over and over. I squeezed all the grace out of that place until at last God disappeared.

"Who are you, O God?" The St. Francis question, with its twin: And, "Who am I?"

Who are you, O God, and Who am I? Who is God, anyway? Who am I in relation to God?

I am a gardener. I am a priest.

Jesus upon the day of resurrection kept disappearing, to everyone. Or, could it have been, their perception of Jesus changed, person to person?

Mary mistook Jesus for a gardener. "They have taken away my Lord and I do not know where they have laid him?"(Jn. 20:13) Maybe a gardener like me. Or, perhaps Mary knew him as gardener at resurrection. Or was he her priest?

Who are you, O God? If not everything, the all in all. As expansive as the universe is wide and as eternal as a single atom divided by half divided by half divided by half . . . divided by half.

WHO DO YOU SAY THAT I AM?

Nine

From Pharisee to Faith
From Blindness to Love

PEOPLE QUITTING MARANATHA BACK in the day were labeled as *damned*. Going to hell, or at least reprobate and living outside of God's will, which was essentially the same as being damned. Jesus is either, "Lord of all or not Lord at all," so if God wanted you "in" the church (Maranatha), and you were to leave, you would be placing yourself outside of God's will. Damned. To be restored, you would need to "repent" and return. The "elders" held God's final word, though they would never admit it, and for some reason, God always wanted members to remain in the church.

My unfortunate sister, Nancy, who had joined Maranatha when I did, was cursed by the leadership as "Jezebel". Jezebel was King Ahab's errant wife, so what hope was there for Nancy? Where was she supposed to find grace? Her unpardonable sin, by the way, was disagreeing with leadership about where she should live.

Maranatha was Pharisaic to the extreme, but most—if not all—institutional religion bends along a broad arc towards a narrow understanding of faith. Institutionalism of faith tends to place the institution over faith, at least it tends to do so across time.[1]

---

1. I will leave it to others to decide whether religious institutions are

I've read stories of priests and bishops who withheld or revoked childrens' first communion because rice was used instead of wheat—all because it is believed Jesus used bread made from wheat at the Last Supper. An absurd result, and so contrary to the nature of Jesus himself, such institutional narrow-mindedness.

Must a person really be baptized as an adult rather than as a child? Must a person believe that Mary was a virgin? Must a person be baptized in the Holy Spirit? Must a person even be Christian, in order to receive the amazing and free grace of God? And what does it mean to be, "Christian?" A follower of Christ? But what if you don't believe in the triune nature of God? What if you believe in the triune nature of God but haven't been born again? What if you *admire* the teachings of Jesus, but don't like church?

Is grace free when strings are attached?

These days I wonder, don't you? Why so many people *believe* faith to be exclusive? To them. When so obviously God shows-up everywhere and at all times? God lives right here. Right here. Right here.

I eventually quit Maranatha; I was 25 when I risked hell. Other family members who'd joined also quit, and over time it became obvious—even to me—that Maranatha was nothing more than a Christian cult. The organization and leadership had become a caricature of Christianity rather than the authentic Christianity they claimed to be and practice. Absurd in so many ways, and precisely the type of religion Jesus railed against. Just ask James, Jesus' brother, what "true religion" means, if not taking care of widows and orphans, or feeding the hungry?

A critical question to me, however, is this: Was God a part of Maranatha? Did Divine Mystery show-up despite our wrong-headedness? Indeed, God is everywhere. God lives right here. So yes, God had to have been there, there with all of us. Leadership included. I had some amazing religious experiences over those years, though the theology rigidified me. Was the thrust of the experience more good than bad? Are those my only choices? Is life a zero-sum game?

---

necessary and/or helpful.

I do know this: had I not had that horrendous experience of binding legalism, I probably would not have wrestled with God who, in turn, wrestled with me. Our wrestling match freed me. Freed, but how would I have learned the low price of grace had I spent the rest of my life trying to pay triple for it?

Turns out, Jesus can be Lord of all—even when Jesus is not Lord of all.

Something about black versus white, about the dynamics of hyperbole to drive meaning home. Legalism, or fundamentalism, you see, is faith by hyperbole. To anyone paying attention, it becomes obvious how illogical earning God's love by extremism or performance is. Life is gift, every breath, and every moment, one more of each than I earned or deserve.

It happened late one night, driving through middle Tennessee for work, five years after leaving Maranatha. I hit a breaking point. I had tried so hard, so very hard for years, to be good. A good Christian, a good person. Not just in Maranatha, but Maranatha magnified my efforts, was hyperbole that pointed out just how being good or doing enough was never going to work.

Some of my feelings—many of my feelings—revolved around the juxtaposition of sexual purity, as I've said. Maranatha—and therefore Jesus—demanded purity to the point of emasculation, or denuding, and I knew that I could never be pure enough, at least not in "that" way. I am bisexual, or perhaps gay—I'm not sure I will ever know which, nor am I sure that it matters, the label—but the underlying angst over my sexuality and lack of the ability to express that natural part of my self—stewed inside me like a pressure cooker. The pressure had grown too great.

So there I was, driving late at night, the pressure cooker about to explode, angry, angry, angry at life and at God, so much so that I began railing at the Creator at the top of my lungs. Fomenting, literally shaking my fist and tempting God: "Fine, if that is what you expect of me, I can't do it. Just send me to hell. Go ahead. Send me to hell." I said it and I meant it. I meant this self-curse so deeply, a childish expression to a Lawgiver whose law is impossible. "I tried and cannot do what is expected. I cannot do what you require, I cannot do I cannot do I cannot do I cannot do. Find someone else. You harsh taskmaster."

Then, even as I finished shaking my emotional fist, just as I gave-up—acknowledging viscerally and perhaps badly that I have absolutely nothing to bring to the table—nothing at all—just as I am without one plea—some divine vacuum sucked all of the oxygen from my essence, leaving me completely without, bereft. And in that instant, in that micro-second, one one one hairs-breadth of eternity, I knew—instantly, completely, and assuredly knew—love. Knew as in the knowing between two lovers, intimately and absolutely.

I did not ask for this second moment of grace any more than I asked for the first. I did not repent of my sins. I did not ask for Jesus to come back into my life. I did not do a single thing other than fight. And quit.

As it turns out, quitters win. It turns out. In Christianity. *Only* quitters win.

Follow me, Jesus said to Peter and James and John. They'd not done a thing to be summonsed. Paul, too, struck blind by light on the Road to Damascus, without request, without giving permission. Indeed, exactly what had Paul done to deserve his grace? Killed Christians, that's what he'd done. What made Jesus think of Paul as an optimal lodge for grace?

Amazing. Or Peter abandoning Jesus on the night before he was crucified? Only his tears of self-annihilation saved him.

"Are you saved?" Why no, and how unattractive of you to remind me. As though I had something to do with it. I reject the premise of the question.

I drove home that night, landing in bed sometime after midnight. Exhausted, but freed. I felt a liberation I'd not known in almost a decade. Because I'd been so busy trying to earn God's love. By quitting, I won.

Ten

Jacob Bests God

Jacob was left alone, and a man wrestled with him until daybreak. When the man saw that he did not prevail against Jacob, he struck him on the hip socket, and Jacob's hip was put out of joint as he wrestled with him. Then he said, "Let me go, for the day is breaking." But Jacob said, "I will not let you go, unless you bless me." So he said to him, "What is your name?" And he said, "Jacob." Then the man said, "You shall no longer be called Jacob, but Israel, for you have striven with God and with humans and have prevailed." Then Jacob asked him, "Please tell me your name?" But he said, "Why is it that you ask my name?" And there he blessed him. So Jacob called the place Peniel, saying, "For I have seen God face to face, yet my life is preserved." The sun rose upon him as he passed Penuel, limping because of his hip. Therefore to this day the Israelites do not eat the thigh muscle that is on the hip socket, because he struck Jacob on the hip socket at the thigh muscle. Genesis 32:24–32 (NRSV)

JACOB BESTS GOD

JACOB WRESTLED WITH GOD and pinned God down. He would not let up until God blessed him. God blessed Jacob while simultaneously tapping Jacob's hip. This God-blessed Jacob walked with a limp the rest of his life.

Who is foolhardy enough to take on the ubiquitous, all powerful, awesome, dynamic, terrifying, invisible and living God? One on one?

I walk with a limp. Many people do.

Jacob was a mousey *mama's boy*. Small and wiry, he was delicate. His mom, Rebekah, would shield Jacob when he needed it most, letting him hide behind her skirt, so to speak. Maybe Jacob had no choice, an overbearing mother to match his own frailty.

His twin brother, Esau, was raw and meaty. He smelled the part, too—gamey, an outdoorsman if ever there was one, he hunted deer for stew. No doubt Esau would butcher the animal himself, blood and sinew, bone and muscle. Wrestling with live and dead animals, Esau became his father's, Isaac's, favorite. A real man's man.

It wasn't that their father did not like Jacob. He did not understand Jacob. He understood Esau, his firstborn; he prized Esau.

WHO AM I?

Despite being just minutes older, Esau was, by tradition, destined to inherit and receive his father's blessing. Esau was his father's first love.

Jacob was instead destined to build his life by scratch, though he did have Rebekah's love.

She felt for Jacob, for whatever reason, and connived a way for Jacob to supplant his brother and inherit his father's blessing. As his father's sight dimmed and the boys grew into men, Rebekah perceived that it was time. Isaac sent Esau to kill a deer and cook venison stew—so he could bless Esau ceremonially—only Rebekah cooked stew, dressed Jacob in musky clothes, put furry skins on his arms, and sent him into his now-blind father to receive Isaac's blessing before Esau returned. Sneaky Jacob, you see, pretended to be Esau and Isaac blessed him.

How could Isaac not distinguish between his sons? And why is it this father had only one blessing to offer?

(As to Esau's birthright as first-born, his inheritance was distinguished from the blessing; Esau stupidly sold it to Jacob for food one day when Esau was famished. Sold his inheritance for a bowl of slop.)

Esau became murderously furious at Jacob when he realized Jacob had tricked their father into blessing Esau, so Jacob—ever true to his nature—fled. He fled to his uncle Laban's house, far far away. As Rebekah's (Jacob's mother's) brother, Laban was twice as sneaky as either Rebekah or Jacob—tricksters all of them.

You see, Jacob fell in love with Laban's second daughter, Rachel. Laban convinced Jacob to work seven years for Rachel's hand in marriage, only he deceived Jacob by slipping Rachel's older sister Leah to Jacob instead—in the honeymoon tent. Jacob performed his marital duty with the wrong daughter, sealing their fate. The next morning, realizing the situation, Jacob confronted Laban, who shrugged his shoulders and promised Rachel to Jacob also, in exchange for seven more years of labor.

Next it became Jacob's turn; he tricked his uncle. While working, he employed Laban's flock to build one of his own. His became larger, making him far richer than Laban. He also fathered twelve sons, the twelve tribes of Jacob, now known as the twelve tribes of Israel for God renamed Jacob to, "Israel," when Jacob decided to return home.

Jacob had grown-up. He was no longer the scrawny boy afraid of his own shadow. He had grown into a man responsible for a large family, rich herd of sheep, and many servants.

By now, Jacob had not yet met God. Yes, he'd dreamt of that stairway to heaven, "Jacob's ladder," with its angels ascending and descending. He was running from Esau at the time, and although God made promises to him, he still knew God only as his father's god, not his own. His grandfather's god, not his own. Faith cannot be inherited. Does not pass from one generation to another. God is never satisfied being known as someone else's god. He wants to become your god. He wanted to become Jacob's god.

So it was, as Jacob crossed the desert running once again—this time from Laban—with his herds of sheep, camels, other animals, great wealth, plus his now expansive family, he began to wonder about his brother, Esau. He remembered how he had tricked his brother out of both blessing and inheritance, and how Esau would have murdered Jacob had he not fled those many years before.

What if Esau still harbored murder against him? What if the two of them were to war, his clan against his brother's? What if Jacob lost his sons? His wives? His animals? His own life?

Jacob strategically broke his camp into two, sending one in this direction and the other in that direction. He camped restlessly alone somewhere between the two, using a rock as a pillow. A rock, and he tensed, writhed and cried out. In his dreams, he faced both Esau and his own deceit. But then, no, it couldn't be Esau. An angel? Yes, an angel, only the angel kept pinning Jacob, but ever the trickster, he would thrash free. Nine lives, and finally, finally Jacob struggled to the top and pinned the angel.

"I won't let you go until you bless me."

Not, "Who are you?" Not, "Why are you wrestling me?" Jacob, still coveting what was not his to own, he demanded blessing. And received blessing. The blessing of God. God blessed Jacob.

"You shall no longer be called Jacob, but Israel."

There was no angel. There never had been an angel, for the angel was God. By pinning God down, Jacob thought he'd won, only God had pinned him. For the first time in his sorry-ass life, Jacob experienced first hand what he'd only heard stories about. The God of Jacob's father and grandfather became his God, intimate and tender.

The next day, Esau accomplished what so few people do in this life. He forgave the unforgivable. He'd heard his brother was returning home so he rushed to meet him. Esau jumped off his horse, grabbed his brother in a bear hug, held him tight, and loved him. Esau *loved* Jacob.

I do not know why God chose Jacob over Esau to generate the twelve tribes. It seems to me that Esau accomplished the greatest of spiritual feats, that of genuine forgiveness of an other. Still, Jacob wrestled the Almighty and pinned her down.

These days, I, too, walk with a limp. My wrestling with God that night along the dark, middle Tennessee road was the only way—the only way—I was ever going to change. And that night, I changed forever. God pinned me, I flung myself against God, and God caught me. And held me. Tightly.

I now know that there is nothing—absolutely nothing—I can do to earn God's love.

Jesus said ever so obliquely, the violent have been taking the Kingdom of God by force.

I've wondered over the years why more people don't wrestle with God. Don't yell at God. Don't seize God by the proverbial collar and say, Why have you done this to me? Who do you think you are? Don't you care?

Like the disciples in the boat cried to Jesus, "do you not care that we are perishing?" (Mk. 4:38) Don't you care that we're going to die?

Faith is not mamby pamby, not some cerebral exercise of wishy washy passivity. Faith is engagement, honest engagement, in whatever form that engagement might take.

"Who are you, O God, and who am I?"

Eleven

The Word of God

Is the Bible the "Word of God?" The book itself, the words in print, the bound sixty-six books of the "Canon of Scripture"? Or could it be that the "Word of God" is something altogether different? Perhaps something invisible, inaccessible unless attended by grace? Rather than ink on paper?

My parents gave me my first Bible the night I was confirmed at the age of eleven, just as I was getting into bed, a King James version with Jesus' words printed in red. The pages were onionskin, the cover black leather, and it closed by zipper with a small brass cross pull.

I do not recall whether they told me they were proud of me for getting confirmed, though confirmation classes were neither rigorous nor spiritual. I had to memorize the Ten Commandments and the Twenty-third Psalm, but I was confirmed with no real understanding of confirmation.[1]

"We want you to have a Bible," they told me.

"Okay, thanks."

---

[1]. My own view is that confirmation is a coming of age rite in which a person has the opportunity to claim faith for themselves.

My father—Daddy—added, "Rob, you ought to read this Bible. One chapter each day is easy enough."

Daddy and I did not get along from the time I was eight or nine years old. By the time I was confirmed at eleven, we were arguing vociferously at dinner most nights, in part due to his strange incarnation as a parent—aloof yet dictatorial, alcoholic, dysfunctional. Still, I craved my father's attention and acceptance, and here he was, offering religious instruction despite being decidedly areligious. If he was spiritual or felt things deeply, I certainly was not aware of it.

That father suggested I read the Bible. Daily.

They kissed me goodnight and left, so I gave it a try. I started reading the red-letter portions, the Jesus books, and from that night forward, I read almost daily, for years, for decades. The habit slowly braided itself into practice over the years, and now, fifty-three years later, reading the Bible still connects me spiritually in a way that almost nothing else can or does.

For years I would read without guidance or instruction, without interpretation, without any real understanding. Then one day, I read that Jesus "opened their minds to understand the scriptures."

(Lk. 24:45) So I prayed, "Lord, open my mind to understand the Scriptures."

Scripture became a plum line, something to teach me and to measure my life by. But, it also—as I said—became a departure point for spiritual connection.

Which leads me back to my original question: "Is the Bible Word?" *The Word of God,* as so many people call it? The same people who wield the Bible as sword against other people, who use the Bible to judge others harshly, who use the Bible to justify their own wayward viewpoint. So let me begin by noting: attacking in the name of something holy does not make the attack holy.

Over the years, I have came to appreciate the Bible as stories of people of faith, distinct from *The Word of* God. These people lived lives like mine, attempting to understand themselves in a world in which awful things can and do happen, to understand themselves and their times in light of a firm belief that there is God—One unseen, behind a veil, but nonetheless engaged intricately in human affairs. In other words, in the Bible I find millennia of people who experienced and interpreted their lives with God in mind. Inspired. Inspiring me to life with God.

That same Bible claims that *The Word of God* is alive, a sword dividing joint from marrow, even names Jesus, *Word*. Many Christians, if not most, claim the Bible to be that very same *Word*. I disagree. The ink on paper is just that: ink on paper. It was never the literal text that mattered, but the spirit behind the text. The wind, the breath, breathing life into the words that are on the paper, just as Spirit breathed life into creation, at the beginning. Only with the breath of God does the text come truly alive. Without the breath of God, the text is merely dead letter. Again, used by people often for their own purposes.

Regarding its spatial nature, the Bible is finite, has a beginning and an end, a start and a finish. Regarding its temporal nature, there was a time in the history of the universe when the words did not exist as they are, then a time when they did. The breath and very *Word of God,* on the other hand, are eternal both spatially and temporally—spatially as they poetically support the universe, and temporally as they have existed from time immemorial.

The Word, you see, is beautifully infinite, unbounded by time or space. Eternal. So no, the Bible as paper and ink are not by themselves holy.

Plus, as so many people have observed, what are we to make of the fact that, over the course of history, there have been those saints who wanted certain writings included while there have been other saints who wanted the same writings excluded? Of course it was men, not women, who took a vote, or perhaps reached a tenuous consensus.

Unbounded, and I learned over time that Scripture—not the words themselves, not the ink on paper, but *The Word of God*—links me to God. As it is written, *the letter kills, but the spirit gives life.* (2 Cor. 3:6) The words of the Bible are valuable only when Spirit animates the words. "Lord, open my mind to understand your Scripture," I would pray.

And so often, as I would read, somehow grace—despite the horrendous stories of murder and mayhem, despite harsh judgment conveyed by ugly words, despite the lives of people who just could never do "it" right—grace emerges. Not from the words themselves, but from the space between the words. God meets me there, in the book itself. Word meets me there, the *feeling* between the words.

If my understanding is correct, then it would be idolatry to treat the ink on paper as *The Word of God,* for the Bible is not God.

Sometimes I wonder about the malleability of the words of the Bible. It seems to become something different to each person who encounters it, according to what a person needs or according to where a person is in their life, spiritually, emotionally and otherwise. The harsh person reads the Bible as judgment against others. The kind person reads it as grace, and in turn offers grace. The person who needs a foundation finds stability, and the spiritual spiritism. I read it as connection, so I feel connected.

Rabbi Levinas, I am told, wrote something along the order of, "rub the page until it bleeds." By that, I suspect he meant that we are not to take the words without thoughtful listening—prayer, study, and spirit.

Scripture. Word. Not dead letter, and not the compilation of stories themselves. The experience of people throughout near-east recorded history that have encountered God as holy and good and perfect, as judge and king and lord. Elohim. El Shaddai. Divine Mystery. Holy One.

Are there other sacred writings in which one might encounter grace? Of course, for God seeks the seeker and loves the lover.

Twelve

Holy Scripture
written in 2009

THE WORSHIP SPACE AT Temple Emanu-el vaults to the sky—it must be as high as it is wide. Two sets of stained glass windows flank the vaulting space, one on the east and the other on the west. The eastern window appears as a colorful sunrise, the promise of dawn, and the western window is subdued, a day well-spent.

The kids and I attended Stefan's bar mitzvah at Temple this past Saturday. Stefan is a friends' son. The chanting of ancient Hebrew psalm and verse enchanted us, the prayers themselves vaulting through the roof to God. At one point, Stefan and the rabbi ceremonially processed through the congregation holding Torah. So moved was I watching both the faithful and other well-meaning people reach out to touch Torah with their fingers as it went by, after first lifting their fingers to their lips. Lips to Scripture in reverence and deep devotion. In devotion to something that is holy, greater than they are, in recognition that it is, as we say in our tradition, "you who has made us, and not we ourselves."

Torah is the Book of Moses, the first five volumes of Hebrew and Christian Scripture: Genesis, Exodus, Leviticus, Numbers and Deuteronomy. Torah is at once revered and controversial—God created, but did God *really* speak magic and create in a literal six days? Law is sacred, but should society *really* slice the hands off of thieves?

The Jewish prayer book I held in my hands during the bar mitzvah read appropriately from right to left and was filled with Hebrew words I do not know. Footnotes at the bottom of pages offered explanations and injunctions. I noticed one particular footnote, as Stefan read Torah to us in Hebrew, that called upon Jews not just to read Torah, but to "engage" Torah, as well.

Engage. As in confront. Argue with. Grow into. Like two people *engaged* to be married, you discover each other, you poke and prod and test each other in order to discover strengths and weaknesses, to change the other by your presence, to be changed by the other in your presence, to strengthen one another. To live with and become a part of. Engage.

We cannot help ourselves. It is almost impossible for us to treat Scripture as something other than black on white page. We are westerners, and written word becomes history or science or some other fact-based information—something to be taken and interpreted literally. No, we Episcopalians do not think of ourselves as Scripture literalists, but our very nature compels us to approach Scripture as something you either accept or reject—and because so much seems arcane or fanciful, we reject it. Or worse—we don't *engage* it. Why would you engage a document that condemns adulterers to a death by stoning?

I'll tell you why: God is lurking between ink and page in Scripture. You meet God, you *engage* God when you engage Scripture, when you treat it reverentially, when it becomes to you *holy*—set apart, special. Rabbi Levinas spoke of rubbing the page until it bleeds—and I add that it bleeds because it is *alive*. Scripture is alive, but few of us discover that fact because we refuse to engage. Like a man and a woman engaged to be married. Scripture engaged becomes the oil lamp and God the genie when you rub the pages, God arising as wisps of smoke from the words to heal and protect and secure you.

WHO AM I?

Thirteen

Exploration

My parents should have placed guardrails around me.

I was four years old. The rest of the family was downstairs: Mom, Daddy, Butch, Nancy and Pete. It was early evening, just before supper.

WHO AM I?

I snuck into my parents' bedroom, *found* matches on their bedside table (they both smoked at the time), and struck a match underneath their bed. I wanted to find out what might happen if I lit the gauze manufacturers staple to the underside of box springs. The gauze caught fire and started to spread. I scrambled to suffocate it, which I managed to do, but I wonder. What if I had not? Put out the fire?

Six or seven years later, I almost electrocuted myself. We lived on Gardenia Lane, in Vero Beach, in the house I consider to be my childhood home. I was just as curious then as I had been earlier, and still experimenting. This time, I took an old extension cord, cut off the end, and stripped the wires bare. I plugged the male end of the cord into the socket and with one wire in each hand, flashed the wires against each other. Again, I wanted to see what might happen. I was vaguely aware of some danger, but how much? I wanted to *see* electricity. I wanted to *feel* electricity.

Later, I learned that you can use a can of Lysol spray as a flamethrower.[1] Light a match while spraying. I also tried jumping off the roof of the garage, to see whether I could fly. I squirt oil all over a neighbor's garage because the oil was there and squirting it was fun. I drank Pine Sol, though I still don't know why I thought that was a good idea.

To be curious, though, is to be human, or to be human is to be curious. Exploring is living. And a child's mind isn't yet bound by convention. Put another way, boys will be boys. Or, girls will be boys, or boys will be girls.

NASA launched its Apollo rockets in those days, and we'd ride our bikes to the beach to watch the rockets rise as daylight stars over the ocean. If launched at night, you could see visceral balls of fire racing through and igniting the sky with aura. Even now, I wonder how anybody survives docked inside balls of fire? To the moon, and beyond, our quest to grasp at meaning, to find God. Years later I took my two children, teenagers, from California to Florida to watch a nighttime launch of the space shuttle. An

---

[1]. I understand this is no longer possible, as fluorocarbon aerosols are banned from use.

astronaut friend invited us—it was one of his launches. Pre-dawn, the orb rose fiery from the launchpad; the night dark became instant sunrise.

And oh, the stars! Who hasn't lain flat on earth staring at stars and wondering at the expanse of it all? Even the Apostle Paul hinted that every person looking up will find God, anybody who wants to. I still trace my fingers across the swath of Milky Way on moonless nights; I did so just two nights ago. Where does it end, and where does it begin? This universe? Infinity within and infinity without. Beyond ourselves, yet so defining of the human soul, there is a fleck of eternity harbored within each of us. Galaxies, space, infinity, right here.

The European explorers, Francis Drake and Ferdinand Magellan; Edmund Hilary; and even explorers today, the girl I recall sailing her little boat around the world, and Shaun White launching a snowboard tall above the horizon. Oh, the physicality of exploration, pushing limits of the human body! Why else would someone climb rocks we call Mt. Everest? Like Teddy Roosevelt, exploring uncharted segments of the Amazon River *after* being president—why, if not to discover that which lies beyond what we see?

Pushing beyond human boundaries *is* exploring God. The Almighty is tucked sideways into cracks and crevices, is found among stars and galaxies, novae and and black holes.

And I have to ask, shouldn't the number one job of the church be exploration? Exploration not just scientifically, but theologically, doctrinally, dogmatically. Why is our religion static, bounded by paper and string, tight like a package sent through the mail?

I once thought that the Holy Book contained the entirety of the universe, and in some ways it does, as God emerges as I've written from between the words themselves. Only, the universe cannot contain the universe, and God cannot contain God. No wonder our primary "sin," if you will, our fault, is creating likenesses of God? Even our Christian law, rules—moral or theological—are prepubescent efforts to contain God. For freedom, Paul claimed, Christ set us free. Bound-less.

WHO AM I?

    For freedom, not to treat others badly, and not to disrespect God. Love God, love your neighbor, those are the bounds of the universe.

Fourteen

I will Never Leave You

Shema. The Lord is our God. The Lord is One. You shall therefore . . . love.

You shall love the Lord your God with all your heart and with all your soul and with all your strength.

The Higgs Boson has been dubbed the "God particle" because it enables mass, providing mass to other matter. As though it might be the origin piece, the most fundamental element of matter that underlies existence.

Of course the so-called God particle is not truly the God particle, not truly the starting point. The Higgs Boson quelled waves into mass, though virtually impossible to observe, while God quelled the deep into universe, black holes, galaxies, earth and sky. Is God the force behind the Higgs Boson? Is the question answerable?

We have this theological concept of the "Trinity," though by definition any description of God, including Trinity, must be inadequate. The concept of the Trinity is at once inexplicable and compelling, mysterious and impossible.

It begins with Shema, the theological God Particle: the singularity of God. Abraham experienced God as singular or unitary at a time when the dominant religious concept was of multiple gods. Abraham's experience of one God was as disturbing to Abraham's world as Copernicus' theory that the earth revolves around the sun was to his. Copernicus is the father of astronomy just as Abraham is the father of three religions based upon the concept of the unitarian nature of God: Judaism, Christianity, and Islam. "The Lord your God is One."

The first Christians encountered Jesus as this man-god. He seemed to be the full embodiment of the One God, both divine and incarnate. Theologically, it would be incorrect to say, "Jesus is God," as Jesus is fully human and thus not fully eternal. The human incarnation of the Divine had a point of beginning, where as the second part of the Trinity hails from time immemorial, eternal. Without wandering too far down a distant wormhole, suffice it to say that we as the church experienced God as Son in this man-God Jesus. God is now understood (by us) as two, yet somehow still One. Father, Son.

Next, Christians encountered and identified the third person of the Trinity, the Holy Spirit, first at Pentecost by fire and wind, and then in retrospect, looking back through the history of faith and identifying the Holy Spirit as wisdom, as *ruach* at creation hovering over the deep, as the soft wind of Elijah. King David was filled with Spirit, as were prophets and others in Biblical times. Even King Saul, so misunderstood, fell into the ecstasy of Spirit. At the event of Christian Pentecost, however, the breeze of God became wind became hurricane, living permanently and mystically within the person of the Christian or as some might say, among the body of the faithful.

God is singular, and yet, God is triune.

Christians have appropriated any number of metaphors to explain this inexplicable and impossible phenomenon, without success. No metaphor is capable of conveying this part of the trinitarian truth: that one hundred percent of the first person of the Trinity is located in the second, and one hundred percent of the second person of the Trinity is located in the first. One hundred percent of the third is also in the first and in the second, and both the second and the first are located completely in the third.

Where you encounter the third, you encounter the first and second. Where you find *Patris,* you find *Filii* and *Spiritus Sanctus.* This conundrum is obviously impossible given our framework and experience of the physical universe, for three distinct individuals to be One. Mystery, something you yield to, you lean into, you give yourself over to, not because you understand, but because you experience.

I have been thinking about this God *being* One recently, but in a way opposite from being expansive, and more in the way of the Higgs Boson, or particle, or fundamental smallness. What if there is such a thing—and I contemplate this not as physical science, but as something spiritual and dynamic—what if there is such a thing as the most fundamental and tiniest particle in existence? Perhaps the Higgs Boson, or more likely something altogether different from or even adverse to how we understand the universe and its constitution? Obviously tinier than an atom with its neutrons and electrons and protons, but think in that direction. Quarks, perhaps, and what constitutes a quark?

I wonder—equally as impossible as the concept of Trinity—whether the sum of God exists impossibly as a whole inside each and every one of these tiniest of particles, tiniest of atoms (so to speak). The totality of God, contained within each, so much so that each atom, each element, each bit of matter or mass or even breath, contains untold numbers of the fullness of God. One hundred percent of God everywhere. One hundred percent of God everywhere.

All the while, God is all the same One. Indivisible.

It would be true, then, as the psalmist claims, that there is no place you can go from God's presence. That God is in the highest of heavens, that God is in *Sheol,* that God is and God is and God is and God is . . . breathe in and breathe out, and there is no way to escape the goodness, for

God is love.

God is with you.

God will never leave you nor forsake you.

And then, what do you do with this ubiquitous nature of a God who exists simultaneously and completely and replete across the chasms? Except to settle down, still the soul, and allow silence to collect you with what is completely beyond and yet completely a part of yourself? Inhale. Exhale. Breathe. Life. God, right here.

"Who are you, O God, and who am I?"

Fifteen

The Rotation of Faith

I am the Alpha and the Omega. The Beginning and the End.

. . . let all who are thirsty come: all who want it may have the water of life, and have it for free.

WHO AM I?

The End of the Earth: Finisterre

Sixteen

Possession

"Who are you, O God, and Who am I?"

You: The Great "I Am." Being. Existence. Yes, *I am*, yet inaccessible absent self-disclosure. *I am*, or as the Hebrew might be interpreted, "I will be who I will be." You (Rob) cannot own me. You cannot contain me.

Isn't that the point of the commandment, *no graven images*? Not even words can contain the Eternal, yet every religion at some level attempts to do exactly that, contain God? Including Christianity? Truth. By definition.

WHO AM I?

Pilate spat at Jesus: "What is truth?" Or as Jack Nicholson said, "Truth? You can't handle the truth."[1]

As though truth were some sort of defined possession—a nut, or an orange—something you might hold it in your hands. Truth?

Jesus declared, "I am the way, the truth and the life," which many Christians confuse to mean that Jesus is the only way, the only truth, the only life. But the emphasis is wrong. The words, "I am," are the words the author John emphasized. Repeatedly, time and again, John placed these words in Jesus' mouth: I am . . . I am . . . I am . . . I am . . . I am the way, the truth and the life.

I am who I am. I will be who I will be . . .

Peter and James and John hiked up the mountain with Jesus where they watched him transfigured by forces outside himself, or perhaps by forces within. Incandescent, they observed Jesus' first and true nature. Then they fell asleep. Then they tried to persuade Jesus to let them build a monument to restrain the moment. A tent, a place of worship, as in a tent of meeting. Like the tabernacle. The revival tent. A way to possess their experience. It could be theirs forever.

How many times have I tried to possess something I've experienced or felt?

---

1. *A Few Good Men*. Directed by Rob Reiner. Written by Aaron Sorkin. Columbia Pictures, 1992.

Seventeen

Control

FOLLOWING MY SO-CALLED BAPTISM in the Holy Spirit kneeling beside Mom at her bed, I became involved in church. In those days, the Episcopal Church hosted weekends called, *Faith Alive!*, during which lay church members—including teenagers—traveled to nearby churches to share their experiences of a living faith with other church members. We did this through public testimony and small groups, evangelically, in order to help people incorporate God personally into their worlds. Hearing other people talk about their faith moves people in ways that rote and uninspired liturgy do not.

I became involved in the *Faith Alive!* ministry as a teenager, traveling myself to any number of Episcopal Churches in Florida and even in Alabama to share my own faith with other teenagers.

Each weekend would open with accessible, evangelical worship, led by guitar or piano, rhythmic gospel songs with repetitive refrains. This type of music pulls at emotions in a way that felt fresh and made so many of the old hymns feel impotent by comparison. "I've Got the Joy, Joy, Joy, Joy down in my heart . . . Down in my Heart to Stay!" Or, "Amazing Grace, how sweet the sound," or "Kumbaya, m' Lord . . ." Two-dimensional, perhaps, but effective.

At the end of those weekends, I would feel restored and renewed, as though I was the object of the faith infusion and not others. I had faith, only I needed more faith. I'd believe, only I could not retain the emotional high the weekends provided. Peter and James and John on the mountain, only you can't house faith. Emotion-based faith is a good starting point, but lasting faith is different.

So many times over the years have I have felt like that poor sap who answered Jesus' faith question: "Do you believe?"

"Yes, Lord, I believe, help my unbelief!"

His was an honest confession of faith, and the question has become ever mine. I believe, Lord, help my unbelief. My cycle of faith, doubt, and faith again. And by faith I do not mean cerebral exercise of some sort, but rather a way in which I would, in fact, lend myself to Divine Mystery, to the reverberations of that voice that had whispered in my ear when I was fourteen. "Come to me, all you that are weary and are carrying heavy burdens, and I will give you rest." (Matt. 11:28)

My life of faith, if you can call it that—the rotation of how much I believed or the quality of my giving myself over to the Divine—is exactly that, a rotation. I believe, yet cannot live with, yet cannot live without, so back I return. Maybe a little better each time. Maybe a little deeper. Or maybe not.

I believe. And I stray. I stray most typically because I—like Peter who when he attempted to walk on water—start looking at the water and imagine how cool I am. Self satisfaction, placing too much confidence in my limited abilities, becomes the stormy waves that pull me under. It is as though I've treated faith as terminable, finite, an object I can hold in my hands. Possess. Faith is not an apple, and God will not be contained.

Moses at the burning bush essentially asked, "Who shall I say is sending me?" I.e., "What is your name?" (See Ex. 3) As though a word with consonants and vowels could possibly explain, define, describe or contain the Eternity of the Universe. God cannot—will not—be possessed. The eternal cannot—will not—be contained by the finite. Even using a word to name God—according to the ancient Hebrew tradition—is forboden—*I will be who I will be.* Even our use of the term, "god," as a name for xxxx, is wholly inadequate and inappropriate, so believed the ancient Hebrew children.

And faith in the abstract—my own faith renewed umpteen times through Faith Alive weekends—and in so other many ways from then to the present—is not faith at all unless and until it encounters life. *I am who I am.* I am not *Who I am.* I am not God. And life is messy—and faith resists containment in any form, particularly in statements of faith, like the Nicene Creed.

Do you believe? Help my unbelief.

And that is where God resides—as it turns out—in my unbelief. When I say I believe—it seems I fail. Or, as Paul tried persuading the Corinthians: "So if you think you are standing, watch out . . ." (1 Cor. 10:12)

Put another way, I experience God when I yield, as opposed to when I am taut and unbendable. While being flexible sounds easy, the fundamental or elemental sin of human nature is the opposite—is that post-Eden posture of taking charge. I like to be in charge. I need to be in command.

Suppose I find myself in trouble, regardless of source. I find myself struggling to swim in a great ocean, with waves pushing around me, swirling and trying very hard to pull me under. I naturally call out for help. A lifeboat arrives—though seldom according to my timetable—and I hop in. The waters calm. I find direction, or whatever I need, and I—to mix my metaphors—take control like Peter walking on water.

Control. Is an illusory state of power or existence that I never truly obtain. Fictional, and I never really have it. Never really get there. This is it, happy and secure. Until... Peter looks at the water lapping against his calves and inching to his knees, his legs buckle. He sinks. He cries out, "Save me."

Like that time Jesus sails with the disciples. He falls asleep. The storm arises crashing waves against the bow of the boat. And the scared desperately shake Jesus awake. "[D]o you not care..." that we are going to die? (Mk. 4:38)

Don't you care?

Don't you care, O Lord, that I'm going to die?

"Be still." Jesus commanded the storm. "Be still." Jesus commanded the disciples.

Who are you, O God, and Who am I? Suppose I delete the, "am I," from the sentence: "Who are you, O God, and Who?" Who?

Eighteen

The Prayer for Honesty

WHEN I WAS A teenager, I started offering what has become a lifelong prayer: "Lord, make me honest with you and honest with myself." I can't say what prompted me to offer this prayer, nor can I say that I have been dutifully faithful to the philosophy behind the prayer. Indeed, I, like most of us I suppose, have had areas of my life that I have hidden or hid from.

Yet, the consistency of the prayer has formed a backdrop for my psychological spirituality, if you will, the promise to God that I will at least attempt, within the best of my ability, to face life and myself honestly. Becoming and being honest can be terribly painful, but in the end, I have come to believe that the *one* thing the Lord requires—beyond doing justly, loving mercy and walking humbly—is for us to become more honestly who we are. To become ourselves, the person God made us to be, whatever that is, whatever that means.

I've realized that perhaps we hide from ourselves, or like Adam and Eve in the garden, from God. We obfuscate, rationalize, excuse, and pretend—and yet, humility, for all its negative press, is no more than becoming who we really are. Who God made us to be.

Isn't it?

WHO AM I?

Nineteen

Certainty

Providence

I AM CURIOUS, ARE certainty and destiny the same thing?

Three times in my life, maybe four, have I known that something was going to happen, that a thing completely out of my control was inevitable.

The first time was when I married Laura. We were dating, and I knew early-on in our relationship that we were going to marry. Not so much as a certainty, but as an inevitability. Marriage between the two of us was inevitable.

Laura had just turned 32 in the spring of 1992, and I was 34, when we went on our first date. She was working on her CPA license, which she eventually obtained, and I was a new lawyer. We'd known each other most of our lives, though not particularly well until the previous year when we started palling around together.

I had asked Laura to date me in January of that year. She told me she would think about it and give me her answer after tax season. She finally said yes and we started dating each other exclusively. By June, I knew we would marry, and sure enough, we married on December 19 that same year. In other words, we dated and were married following a short eight-month courtship and engagement.

I've written our story elsewhere, but suffice it to say, becoming close friends first made dating easy and natural. And, even though our short dating life hit a serious bump or two, I knew by the end of that second month that we would marry. My asking her, and her saying yes, were not exactly anticlimactic—she exclaimed to the wait person at the restaurant where she took me to dinner for my birthday, minutes following my proposal, "I'm engaged!" She thrust her engagement ring in the woman's face. Great joy, and it felt then as though our lives had been gilded with destiny.

The thing is, I don't particularly believe in destiny, or at least not in pre-destiny. I tend to believe in inevitability. With grace. And Providence, in the classical sense. Only, using the term, *Providence*, hints at destiny, as in the guiding hand of God in human affairs.

And, I do believe in the guiding hand of God in human affairs. I just don't particularly believe in destiny. Yes, God is involved in human affairs, both great and small—because God cares and because God can be. The problem arises because God cannot be involved in human affairs to the extent it quashes what we think of as "free will." I had the option, and so did Laura, of saying, "No." And yet, I knew . . .

One has to wonder, is there really such a thing as free will? I am, after all, bound to the earth by gravity, regardless of what I'd like to do about it, regardless of my desire and will to fly. I have limited resources, limited brain and spirit power, limited authority over my physical boundaries. Yes, God leaves us to make choices, just within bounds.

It was by destiny that I became a priest. My personal spiritual and emotional struggles—throughout my life—have made me a better priest. For example, wresting myself free of the demon called "Maranatha." Does that mean Maranatha was part of my destiny? That Providence *led* me to a religious experience that left me with such an awful emotional hangover? Yet, struggles offer each of us the opportunity to become a more human being. Are struggles ordained by God? Did the *Spirit* not lead Jesus into the wilderness? Or did life lead Jesus? Are our struggles simply a natural part of being human? Could we not learn by observation rather than experience? Of course we could, and I like to think I could have learned about grace without having experienced the noose of legalism.

I was destined to marry Laura—at least in a certain way—though I suppose I could have married someone else. Does that mean our marriage was not destiny, even though it *was* destined? She could have said, "No, thank you very much," but she said, "Yes!" Thus, my knowing ahead of time was merely foreknowledge, but is such foreknowledge destiny? The destiny of Providence?

I wonder how much all of this has to do with the finite world in which we live. My physical bounds are defined. I *am* fenced-in not just by spatial limitations—like I said, I cannot fly—but also by temporal limitations. I have a beginning and I will have an end, a time to be born and a time to die. Still, God is eternal—so much so, as I've said, that even calling God, "God," violates the eternal and existential nature of the Divine. No word can contain God. My breath cannot contain God. God is before time and after time, in that Augustinian sense, with all of life and all of history about which we know and experience bounded by limits that God exceeds. A breath, and it is all done, has all happened. God has foreknowledge because God is eternal, and all that will happen has already happened. And certain things that fall within the Providence of God are inevitable.

Take grace, for example. At the moment humanity "sinned"—as expressed in the Garden of Eden mythology—there appeared law and grace, instantly and simultaneously. Judgment and hope. Accountability and an open jail cell. In other words, whatever Jesus accomplished on the cross and by his resurrection—which is still a mystery, though theologians from the time of Christ forward have tried in vein to explain—was more inevitable than was my marriage to Laura. God was already bound by time and space to become one of us to somehow rescue us. From sin? From death? From darkness? Grace permeates history—hence the word, "Providence."

As I said, marrying Laura was not the only time I've experienced foreknowledge. At the time, I questioned whether my decision to move from Maryland to California as a widowed single father raising two children was a good one, or even God's call. Yet, I knew that it was going to happen.

Christ Church in Sausalito needed a new rector. Their final choice was between me and a priest from Colorado. As I understand it, some members of the search committee and vestry wanted to call me, and others wanted to call the other priest. The senior lay volunteer, whose title is, "Senior Warden", kept calling me to ask questions. For example, they were worried that, if called, I would expect the parish to help me raise my kids. (Why they thought this is beyond me, but they relayed this concern nonetheless. I laughed. After Laura died, I had only one intent, and that was to be the best parent to my two children that I could be. I did not expect others to raise them.)

Regardless, during that long deliberation process, something I hesitate calling "discernment," I became concretely aware that Christ Church was going to call me and I would answer the call by moving my children to California from Maryland. I sincerely doubt that God removed the decision from the search committee and vestry, or from me, though I do believe God knew what we all would decide. For some reason still unknown to me, divine foreknowledge was shared with me. I knew.

CERTAINTY

I had a similar experience when called to return to serve my home parish in Knoxville, Tennessee, the Church of the Ascension. I knew I would be called. And, for the third time in my life, I found myself in Tennessee: I had been born there (and baptized as a baby at Ascension), returned for law school (and worshipped at Ascension), and finally returned to serve Ascension. Each time as an adult—and maybe I will write about this later—I discovered that the city I thought would be "home" for me was not that at all. Did God call me back to Knoxville, or did God simply tell me where I was headed?

Is God nothing more than a crystal ball revealing some inevitable path?

Foreknowledge and destiny, Providence and predestination. Free will and choice. I would be remiss to offer an explanation, but what I come back to is this, that God is with us each and every step of the way, whether in or out of whatever the "will of God" might happen to be. *"I will never leave you nor forsake you,"* never, never, never, and the grace of God holds us tenderly, even when the choice is ours, even when decisions are out of our hands, even when we have no choice at all. Because in the end,

God is good, all the time, and all the time, God is good.

Twenty

Guidance
Holy Spirit

NONE OF WHAT I write about Providence and certainty is to say that God as Holy Spirit does not guide, which she does.

One day, serving as priest in Maryland, I had an "inkling" to telephone a particular young family that attended church, though infrequently. I'd not spoken to them other than at church and had not called on them before now. The young father answered the phone.

"David, it's Rob, at the church," I announced, to which he responded in tears. "Oh, Rob. Thank you for calling. We just got home. I ran over our dog in the driveway. Just now. He's dead."

Unbelievable, that I should call within minutes of their tragic incident. Was the instinct to call happenstance? Or the guidance of grace? Our conversation continued pastorally, ending in a prayer of solace and faith.

I believe in the guidance of the Holy Spirit, just as I believe in other workings of the Holy Spirit, an internal guide and/or prod. I cannot tell you how many times I've felt a holy impulse at just the pivotal moment for myself or someone in need. Again, *God is good, and all the time.*

Likewise, I cannot tell you how many times I have resisted the same sacred impulse, and someone has gone without care because I failed. And again, *God is good, and all the time.*

Twenty-One

Love

Love. What is love, I wonder?

Is it an emotion? A state of being? An action? Something tangible, or esoteric? Ethereal? Does love swirl about as a cool breeze about the head?

Can love be idle? Or must it be moving in order *to be*? Can love live without a donor or can it live without an object? As in, abstract, like the Zen køan, *one hand clapping*, does it need the second?

If James is correct, that faith without works is dead, is love not also dead? Without works, without movement, object, or objective? What is love unexecuted except a balloon without air?

If "God is love," (1 Jn. 4:8), does that mean God exists only in the movement towards something or someone?

The assertion itself, *God is love*, suggests that love *is* existential, an object or movement without object. But, can the corollary be true? Could you say, "*Love is God?*" Or, would that make an idol of love? If God is love and love is not God, then God cannot be love, or so it might seem.

Certainly, though, love is movement, and God as love suggests movement. As in, love swirling about the godhead, the Trinity, one member expressing love to the Other, giving itself to the Other, preferring the Other, so much love that the movement explodes outward in the form of creating. Love creating, and love cannot *not* create, which is how the Creator became the progenitor of the world, as love is poured upon the Other and the Other, like water across the feet. *Love*. By definition, is self-giving, or the giving of self.

Still, love is not an object to be studied, it is poetry to be felt.

Paul waxes poetically of love when trying to convince that fractious group of Christians, the Corinthians, to treat one another in love. Do not think more highly of yourself than you ought. Esteem the other. Do not demand your own way.

Do not demand your own way. Yet, we Christians can be so demanding, and love so poorly. Consider these dogmatic positions:

- Only a "believer's baptism" works salvation.
- You must observe the Sabbath, which is Sunday, not the Jewish Saturday.
- You must observe the Sabbath, which is Saturday, not the Christian Sunday.

- You are not allowed to bless the bread and wine as sacrament unless you are ordained in the Petrine line of succession.
- *Sola Scriptura,* or Scripture Only, and no other sacred writing conveys grace.
- Doctrine upon doctrine, and creed upon creed, and can any human being really say whether the Holy Spirit proceeds from the Father alone, or from both the Father and the Son?
- And when did God become male, anyway?

Love. As in Bert Kaempf and Milt Gabler's tune , "L is for the way you look at me . . ."[1]

Love does not demand its own way, does not notice when others do it wrong—is family when family is done right. A hearth, a place of security, to which you return at the end of a long day, to feel at home. And aren't we all seeking *home?*

Home is where the small are great and the great are small. The small are great, and this is where I begin to think of Jesus' command to love my neighbor as myself. How can I say that I love God whom I cannot see when I do not love my neighbor whom I see? Love—as in the person next to me—is great. As God is great.

I met a fellow once who had been married three times. His first two marriages ended in divorce. He was in his seventies, now on his third marriage, for just over a year then. He'd heard I was a priest, so he cozied up to me at a party. "I can help you with your couples getting married. I can tell them what they need to know."

Doubtful, his offer seemed arrogant, I nonetheless responded politely, "Really . . . How?"

"Well," he said, "I finally learned. During my first two marriages, I would wake up every day subconsciously imagining, 'What can my wife do for me?' Now I wake up every day asking the opposite, 'What can I do for my wife?'"

What can I do for her? As in, prefer the *other.* Do not insist upon your own way. And, does it matter anyway whether a person

---

1. Bert Kaempf and Milt Gabler, writers, "L-O-V-E," performed by Nat King Cole, recorded June 3, 1964, track 1 on *L-O-V-E,* Capitol.

is baptized as an infant or after the age of reason? Where and when do we suppose God shows-up, anyway? If not in the little kindnesses we show to another. The foundation of ritual, shouldn't it be love, and not doctrine?

Pastor Steven Furtrick of Elevation Church regularly touts, "Love is not words, it's actions, and love isn't feelings, it's a decision."

Love, an action verb.

And yet, love is the posture of the soul, the bend of the soul, the soul's orientation. Am I oriented towards love, or towards judgment? Do I lean into love?

Christians are like everybody else in the world. We get frustrated and angry. Being human, everyday life, and it seems more and more as though loving my neighbor as myself is near-impossible. It is easy to love God, for God first loved me. Love begat love, but how do I love someone who doesn't love me in return? If God did not love me first, would I still love God? Yet, that is what Jesus as Christ ordered, his second commandment subsuming the first.

Love is not a choice, and yet it is every bit a choice.

During winters, I work on a ski mountain as a mountain guest host. Our boss constantly reminds us to be nice—always nice—to the guests. Some guests, though not many, clearly feel entitled, and we all know what that means. When angry, these people have been known to spit epithets into our faces, as hosts. Of course, being "nice" does not mean taking abuse. Loving others does not mean living as a pin cushion. Still, I find it easier to treat such guests well when I, myself, assume an interior posture of joy. When I am enjoying my day, my work, rejoicing in the graces given to me. On the other hand, when my fundamental posture changes, when I feel myself in the midst of a "bad" day, I become frustrated, even angry, eroding my "niceness" or kindness, my expression of love. Orientation is everything, including as a choice we make.

Be kind.

Love. John writes, "We love because [God] first loved us." (1 Jn. 4:19) I am so deeply grateful for the love that introduced me to grace, and reintroduced me to grace, and each new day awakens me to more grace, so much so that the love of God is shed abroad in my heart, as the writer claimed . . . and that is the direction to which I incline myself. I lean into love.

Love, though, is more than just posture, and more than mere decision, and more, even, than grace.

I learned more about my own depth of love when Laura died. That very same day.

She'd had gallbladder surgery in the afternoon, and the hospital released her that night rather than keep her. They instructed her to resume her hefty pain medicine regimen, necessary due to her longer-term illness by which pain dominated her body, despite my feeble protests. "Are you sure? Do you realize how much pain medicine she takes?" I asked, knowing she'd just undergone gallbladder surgery that included anesthesia, and who knows what other heavy drugs might still be in her system? Her system had been further compromised because she'd eaten very little in two weeks, due to the gallbladder issues. She was weak.

"We have it all right here," the discharge nurse responded. "The doctor says she's to continue her regular medications." Laura died in her sleep that night following surgery. Her weakened system gave out.

The following night, after a day of caring for two young children whose mom has just died and giving Laura's dad the worst news of his life, as I lay in bed just realizing the full extent of my own loss, I understood something about love that I'd never known before. Or maybe I *felt* something about love. Mine was not an emotional realization, nor any type of Hallmark sentimentality. Rather, it was this, something I've heard repeated since by others who have lost their spouses: I felt as though a part of me had gone missing. That someone had cut off my arm and left me reduced. My loss was the loss of love, love halved. Bifurcated.

Love, then, is organic, the braiding of lives together, as in the two become one.

I wonder, then, what it means to love those whom you do not know? The woman next to you on the subway, or the man who cuts in front of you at the grocery store? The person on the ski slope who shouts epithets? How do I love, if I do not appreciate the unseen, unknown ways in which we are connected? That the two become one, and that at some perhaps microcosmic level, what I do affects her life? For good or for ill? That I am a part of him, and he of me. That person I do not know.

Interconnectedness, and think of that. God exists everywhere simultaneously, which means that in the end none of us can own God. At best, any piece of our doctrinal view of God—regardless of denomination and even religion—is fractional. I need the *other* to complete me. I always need you. As Paul writes to the same Corinthians, "The eye cannot say to the hand, 'I have no need of you...'" (1 Cor. 12:21)

Even the word, "interconnectedness," is insufficient, impotent. Suppose—just suppose—that the entirety of humanity—the whole—is itself just one living organism, like a stand of aspen or redwood trees, all a single plant. Or, that all of life's breath, animals included, comes from the soul of one living compound organism?

In you we live and move and have our being. The breath of God, the *Ruach,* hovering over the deep at creation, the same breath that fills my lungs with the oxygen of hope is the same breath of hope that is in you. In and out, in and out, in and out, and my lungs are filled with the grace and mix of commonality and individuality. How can that be, but by love?

What is love? Love is—well, love is *love*. Indefinable, you know it when you see it, when you feel it, surprising, and always new, *love*. Poetry, not substance.

Twenty-Two

The Sea Vista, I

WE MOVED TO VERO Beach from Tennessee in 1964, to the Sea Vista Motel. I was five, about to turn six. My father started his adult life as a civil engineer, became a stockbroker, and now a motel owner and manager. The Sea Vista was one of those old Florida art deco motels—turquoise—located just south of South Beach. In the lobby of the Sea Vista, my father kept a cage of finches, and at Christmastime he would decorate a small aluminum tree with color wheel.

We lived in the owner's suite just off the lobby, tiny with only two-bedrooms, a living area and small kitchen. The four of us kids—all under nine—shared the second bedroom, sleeping in bunkbeds. One night Daddy was putting us to bed, sitting next to me on the bottom bunk. The bunk jarred, and the top bunk started to fall. It might have crushed me, but Daddy caught it, saving me.

I don't recall that incident often, and most memories of my father are unpleasant. But, he gave me life, and then he saved me. Then later, he gave me that King James Bible and told me to read it. Not bad, only I coveted more. I wanted to be noticed, I needed his esteem. I needed to learn from him. A boy needs his father. Only, we never played ball, golfed, or chatted. Mostly, I felt as though I was in his way, and I probably was.

During the busy winter season at the Sea Vista, Mom and Daddy would throw parties for the guests. Guests in those days were long-term residents, snowbirds from the north who would stay all winter. Florida was not yet jammed with condos. The beaches were still wide and empty.

To keep us occupied during their parties, Mom would give us a can of Crazy Foam and send the four of us kids into the small bathroom to take a bath, four kids in one tub. The consistency of Crazy Foam falls somewhere between shaving cream and whipped cream. We would squirt Crazy Foam at each other, use it to make beards, then smear it on the pink tiles. Hours in the tub alone, and during all those parties we never fought, nor did we drown.

One year, a hurricane grazed Vero Beach. The power went out and Mom couldn't cook, so Mom and Daddy took us across the street to eat dinner at the Menu Restaurant. I remember crossing the street, the ocean at our backsides. The wind and rain pelted us fiercely from the west, so we leant into the storm. The door to the restaurant flew open wide when Daddy pulled at it, and there they were, the lovely French couple who had emigrated to the States after the war to rebuild their lives, welcoming us as their only patrons that night. My own parents had lived in France when they first married and my dad loved escargot, which he ordered. I ordered frogs' legs, for the novelty of it, and because I loved the taste of garlic with butter. That couple became my parents' friends, and we'd eat at the Menu whenever someone would visit us from Tennessee.

We had all kinds of pets in those days, including frogs—Florida toads, not at all like those I ate at the Menu. You could find those toads in every ditch at the right time of the year. Dogs and cats, too, plus fish and turtles and tadpoles. A parrot named Thornton, an iguana, and even a cayman alligator.

So many pets, that naturally when the baby sea turtles hatched on the beach, and crawled westward instead of east towards the ocean like nature and God intended, we kept one. Nobody knew back then that the turtles follow the light from sunrise eastward into the ocean. Lights from our motel led them onto the motel property where we found them everywhere. Under bushes, in the swimming pool, behind rocks. This was 1966, before we knew to protect sea turtles, before the federal government enacted protection laws, and long before any dark sky movement. As we collected the turtles, we'd take them to the surf to set them free and send them on their way.

Like I said, we kept one of the babies as a pet for a week, until Mom finally told us it was time to set him free. We took him out past the breakers and gently guided him into the deep.

Of course he probably died. Most of the baby turtles, if not all of them, would have died. Very few make it to maturity anyway, and these little guys would have expended what little store of energy they had from gestation chasing the lights, toddling in the wrong direction. They needed every ounce of energy to swim past the surf, find food, and escape predators.

They say that, when the time comes, a sea turtle will return to its birthplace to lay eggs, like salmon. How does a turtle know where to swim? What embedded compass do they have that we lack? Or do we have a compass? After all, I returned to Tennessee, to my birthplace, when I became an adult.

Or, do we lack direction? Or could some embedded GPS be guiding us along the way, to home of hearth and heart?

St. Augustine referred to a spiritual notation written in the margins of each of us, a homing device, a God-sized hole needing to be filled. We won't be satisfied until it is filled with God, he wrote.

I recently finished reading a novel that emphasized science over religion, fact over faith, but I wonder why the author treated the question as binary, either/or? Why in the sixteenth century did the Roman church feel so threatened by Copernicus that they excommunicated him? As though science contradicts rather than complements our understanding of the world?

Either we are spiritual beings or we are not, either there is a god or there is not.

Why do so many people of faith—and I do not mean just Christians—treat their faith as something to guard and protect rather than to liberate and explore? A faith that does not free a person is not faith, but irons. Faith—true faith—makes a person more fully human. If not, why bother?

People were born and bound godward as the turtles for the sea, only we seem misguided toward land by a false sunrise. Though misdirected, will we find strength for the journey?

Twenty-Three

The Complexities

My relationship to my father is both simple and complex. It is simple because he died when I was eighteen, and it is complex because I seldom—if ever—received the love from him that I desperately wanted and needed.

His dying at forty-five, when I was just eighteen, was a reduction: his death made our relationship simple, for one *simple* reason. For years, he and I fought viciously, nightly over dinner, usually about petty matters. This dynamic started when I was about nine years old. Our pattern, our way of being, became indelible and immutable across the years, until his death. His dying enabled me to take our relationship, stick it in a metaphoric shoebox and place that box on the back shelf of my psychological closet. From that shelf I could pull it down, dust it off, open it, and examine it at my leisure—or during a crisis when I desperately needed to figure parts of my life out.

The complexities of our relationship are not difficult to explain, but tangled. Some of the information I learned later about my father might be completely inaccurate as supposition and hearsay. However, my father, like so many alcoholics, surely drank to hide something from himself and likely others, perhaps some event.

THE COMPLEXITIES

My father played jazz piano—by ear, and exquisitely. He cut his teeth by sneaking out of his parents' house in Memphis as a teenager to run off to Beale Street. There he listened to and learned the art of jazz jam. He drank alcohol in those days, according to my uncles, something he started as early as nine or ten years old. Copious amounts, too, certainly damaging and altering his brain chemistry and development.

I used to wonder why Daddy couldn't stop drinking when other alcoholics could, figuring he just didn't want to. He certainly had more opportunity than most; he enrolled in any number of detox programs (mostly at my mother's insistence). They never took, and I now realize that starting to drink so young, he probably couldn't stop—physiologically. His brain chemistry and constitution had become so altered that for him, there could never be life without alcohol.

In January of 1977, when I was a freshman in college, doctors rushed Daddy from Vero Beach to Jackson Memorial Hospital in Miami, where the doctors told him plainly, "You will die within six months if you do not stop drinking." He quit for just one month, resumed drinking, and died in August. In Minneapolis.

Mom had enrolled Daddy in yet another treatment program, this time at St. Mary's Hospital. St. Mary's was one of the first facilities in the country to treat alcoholics using "intervention". Intervention meant that family and close friends would confront the alcoholic about how his or her drinking affected them. The intent is to hold a psychological mirror up to a person so they can see how damaging their drinking is to others, thus giving them incentive to quit. Drinking is, after all, a family tragedy, affecting everyone in the alcoholic's orbit, and not just the alcoholic herself: a family disease.

We dutifully gathered in Minneapolis for that purpose. My sister Nancy left summer school at the University of Florida to fly-in. My two brothers, Butch and Pete, flew in from Vero, and I came over from Yellowstone where I held a summer job following my first year in college. Together, with my mother—who was already in Minneapolis—we confronted Daddy.

We confronted him with the horrors of living with him as drunk, but I—it was always I who was in the family hot-seat—spoke the most and the loudest. I broke down telling my father how awful the years had been for me, his constant state of drunkenness and our constant fighting. I reminded him of the times I had to drive him around town, even as early as twelve years old, without a license, because he was too drunk to drive. I complained about his falling face down in the driveway seemingly every day while I was in high school, just steps from the front door, bloodying his arms and face.

I recently read a memoir by William Glenn whose paternal dynamic sounded eerily familiar.[1] He writes that he has the gift (or curse) of being able to see into others' souls (my words, not his), to know what is going on. Just by his presence he mirrors peoples' souls to them, which can be hard and feel confrontational to the person on the receiving end. In his own confrontations with his father, he believes he projected his father's darkness back to him. His father became resentful and hostile in a way that he was not hostile to the other children in the family.

I identify with that description, at least the part in which my father likely saw his own darkness through me. I am not sure I saw or intuited what was going on inside of him, and my "gift" is different from William Glenn's. My gift—or curse—is that I react to injustice or imbalance, and I try to address it. When things my father would say or do would not make sense, or more particularly, would feel unjust, I would object. When my brother would eat his meatloaf and not his peas, my father would get angry at him, and I would object. When my father would insist that I say, "Yes sir," instead of a simple, "Yes," I would object. When we were told to pass the pepper with the salt, and neither by itself, I would object. Were his demands reasonable?

One time, probably Thanksgiving because we were using the good silver, my father got angry at me or all of us, banged his knife on the side of the table as hard as he could, and the knife broke in half. The stainless steel blade flew into the air, leaving my father holding the sterling handle. Broken knives, and broken lives.

My point is this. I would not let my father get away with stuff, but opposition cost me dearly. And, the love I craved was the love I was never going to receive. My sister, Nancy, as an only daughter and my dad's little girl, always felt my father's love. My younger brother, Pete—perhaps. My older brother, Butch, with his mental

---

1. Glenn, William D, *I Came Here Seeking a Person*, Mahweh, NJ, Paulist Press, ©2022.

challenges, not so much.[2] And me—never. Moreover, mine became the voice of the family, for better or for worse.

When William Glenn writes that each child perceives a particular parent differently, I agree. I've spent years unravelling my relationship to my father, while my sister, I believe, has spent years unravelling hers to our mother. She felt our father's love in ways that I never did.

Eventually I learned to place the blame where it belonged, which is to say, not on myself. Perhaps there should be no blame, Daddy also being victim of sorts. Still, I was the child, and he was the adult. But, did he ever have a chance? A real chance in life?

"Why couldn't you just keep your mouth shut?" My sister has asked me repeatedly over the years. Only, keeping my mouth shut would have been as unnatural as capping a geyser. I'm the most verbal of the four of us, and the fact that I didn't stifle my emotions served me well in the end. I've been able to process—by talking, complaining, crying, and even writing. Not so much my siblings, who kept it all in and battled some form of alcoholism themselves over the course of their lives. Nancy has been sober now for decades, having faced her own challenges, as was Butch before he died.

Nonetheless, as a teenager, I blamed myself for our bad relationship, my father's and mine. It took years to stop blaming myself and learn that he—and not I—was the parent, the adult, in the room.

It took even more time to appreciate the complexities of human nature, to stop blaming Daddy, to realize that, like I said, he never really had a chance, taking to drink so early. Even more complex, we pieced his puzzle together twenty-five or so years after he'd died, perhaps his dark hole. Daddy may have been complicit in the death of a man on the Mississippi River, probably a Black man. Not necessarily a racist death, though my father certainly was Memphis racist.

My grandfather was a civil engineer, a colonel for the Corps of Engineers, responsible for dredging the Mississippi River at

---

2. "Butch," named "Paul," after our dad, was mentally challenged—"slow." He died in late 2020.

Memphis. As colonel, he hired two of his three boys when they were in their late teens for summer work on the barges. My dad played poker—earned college spending money by gambling. One night, while on or off the job on the barge—who knows?—one of the Black fellows playing cards with them was (and this is my guess) accused of cheating and thrown overboard into the Mississippi. He could not swim and drowned.

My father never shared this story with us and we know it only by piecing together the puzzle with added supposition. My father, near the end of his life, told my mom he had killed someone, something she never shared with any of us until my sister shared her piece of the puzzle with Mom. "Daddy told me," she disclosed, "that he hoped I'd never have to go through what he'd been through." The intimation was that he'd done something unforgivable and hated himself for it. Two plus two equals four. And, something in what he said to one or both of them led to supposition about a drowning on the Mississippi.

Pete, my younger brother, called me one day to tell me the puzzle pieces. "Have you talked to Mom or Nancy?" He asked.

"No, why?"

"They think they've figured something out about Daddy."

"He killed someone." I answered.

"How did you know?" Pete asked.

"I don't know. Is that it?"

"Yes. How could you know?"

I had no way of knowing, yet I somehow knew. Mine was not some flippant guess. I don't know how I knew. I have wracked my brain over years wondering. Did my grandmother tell me? Mim was my father's mother, and I was always close to her. Only, she never would have told me something like that, even had she known it to be true. Imagining she would be maintaining family dignity, she would have kept the secret secret. Did my father tell me during one of our late night chats that last year of his life? (The only time in my life we related to each other was the summer before I started college. He would be close to sober by the time I would arrive home late at night from my job at McDonald's, and we talked then more like adults than a father and child.) No, I would have remembered clearly had he told me.

I dreamt it. Or intuited it. Or made it up. Who knows? Although I do believe that just behind the veil resides the Holy Spirit full of awareness and knowledge, and by the time in my life Pete called me to tell me what he suspected, I knew there must be more to my father than just an insurmountable and unforgivable addiction to alcohol. I just didn't know what that might be.

That is the perennial question: was there more to my father than I, as a child, could have known? Understanding is important to forgiveness. Can you forgive others when you do not know the entire story? Of course you can, but knowing the back story certainly helps.

Forgiveness has been an important hinge to my own spirituality, and of course we all have people to forgive. Deeply, and from the heart.

As to my father, forgiveness has been a process. I have forgiven him twenty times over, or as Jesus quipped, seventy times seven. I no longer hold his infractions against him. Any forgiveness I have mustered has required honest appraisal. He was not a good parent to me, I needed more. But and also, he was not a good person to himself, he needed more. And, I, as a son, must have been a challenge for him.

Four or five years ago, I drove through Memphis on my move back west. I decided to visit Daddy's gravesite, set alongside that of my grandparents and other more distant family members. It was the first time I'd visited his grave in forty years—not once since he'd died had I made the pilgrimage, even though I'd visited Memphis many times. There it was, a flat headstone. I knelt in front of it, placed my palm upon it, and said the words aloud that I'd only said in my heart before. "I forgive you."

Forgiveness is a spiritual posture, necessary, and I would add the most difficult spiritual posture I've ever had to assume. Always on my knees.

And not just my father, but Pete, my brother, and others, as well.

Twenty-Four

Sincerity

IN HIS NOVEL, *My Father's House,* Joseph O'Connor tells the story of an Irish priest stationed at the Vatican during the German occupation of Italy. The priest, Monsignor Hugh, manages a group of volunteers running an underground system to evacuate people endangered by the occupation—escaped prisoners, Jews, and others. The head of the German occupation is Paul Hauptmann, brutal and violent. Brutal and violent, and the Monsignor and Hauptmann become essentially enemies, not only on opposite sides of the war, but on opposite sides of humanity.

Years later, Hauptmann asks the Monsignor to visit him in prison, which he reluctantly does. Over the course of nine visits, Hauptmann ingratiates himself to Hugh, though Hugh never fully trusts Hauptmann's sincerity. He writes in retrospect, "I suppose it should never begin to surprise us that the murderer wears a mask. Yet it does. We all of us wear so many, of course."[1] Still, Hauptmann converts to Catholicism, participates in catechism, and is baptized. This all might sound like a conversion, but Monsignor Hugh doesn't believe it, at least not fully, which is why when Hauptmann asks Hugh to hear his confession, the Monsignor

---

1. O'Connor, Joseph. *My Father's House,* New York, NY, Europa Editions, © 2023, pp. 348–49.

declines. Is he confessing to impress the parole board? Or with integrity? Does it matter? How can a priest—any priest—forgive a man who has committed so many unpardonable—hundreds, thousands of murders—sins?

Twenty-Five

The Hardest Love

A. THE BASICS

The Lord's Prayer: "forgive us our trespasses as we forgive..."

Jesus' explication on the Lord's Prayer: "...if you do not forgive others, neither will your Father forgive your trespasses." Forgiveness begets forgiveness, so it seems. (Matt. 6:15)

Jesus also told his followers that whoever sins you retain, they are retained. Madeline L'engle quotes Eugene Peterson's The Message in his interpretation of Jesus' assignment regarding the retaining of another's sins: "Whatever will you do with them?"[1]

Forgive others.

Or, not. Hold onto wrongs. Yours or others'. Block the freeflow of spirit. Inhibit. Bind. Choke.

I find forgiving others from the heart to be the most difficult exercise of the Christian faith. Forgiveness takes courage.

What is forgiveness? What does it mean to truly forgive another person from the heart? I suppose it might be helpful to consider a few basics regarding forgiveness that I've come to

---

1. L'Engle, Madeleine, *Bright Evening Star*, Colorado Springs, CO, Shaw Books, © 1997, p. 41.

experience over the years, starting with two lists, first of what I believe forgiveness typically is not, and second of what I suspect forgiveness includes.

Forgiveness is not

An Emotion. It is a spiritual choice, one that begins deep inside when the spiritual intuition prods you that it is time to allow grace to heal deep wounds.

Instantaneous. Forgiving others is often a lifetime project. Do not be surprised that it takes time.

Healing. Forgiveness does not mean the person doing the forgiving walks away unscathed, spiritually or psychologically. Injuries leave scars and we all have scars caused by others.

A Resolution. Forgiveness does not mean matters are resolved, relationships are healed, or disparate viewpoints become aligned.

A Denial of Responsibility or Injustice. Forgiveness does not mean that a person who wrongs someone avoids accountability, by society or otherwise. Often, a person forgiving must let go of the demand for justice, but justice may need to be accomplished, depending upon the circumstances. Accounts are not necessarily settled by forgiveness.

Easy. As said, forgiving others is one of the hardest things a person can do.

Continued Entanglement. Forgiveness does not mean that a person is required to continue in or maintain an unhealthy relationship. For example, a person need not continue in a dysfunctional relationship to their detriment, particularly when the other parties to the relationship continue dysfunctional behavior.

Forgiveness

Is a Process. Often, though not always, forgiveness takes time and intention. Letting go might happen like the peeling an onion, one layer at a time.

Means Letting Go. Of the need for retaliation and/or vengeance, and sometimes justice.

Frees the Soul. Emotionally, from the bonds of hate and entanglement. Frees to love.

Can Be by Emotion. Sometimes a person feels ready to let go; feels enough love in the heart; or feels finally forgiveness of self enough to let go.

Is Usually a Choice. Often, one must often choose to forgive, believing forgiveness to be the better way. When someone chooses to forgive, that person can grow into actual forgiveness over time.

Often Takes Time. It is almost impossible to forgive egregious wrongs immediately. Time heals, and forgiveness is, more than anything, a healing process.

Often Requires Understanding. One element to forgiveness is understanding, when a person becomes the other, puts himself into the position of the other and tries to understand what makes that person who they are. Walk a mile in the other person's shoes.

I have been hurt many times over the course of my life, sometimes deeply. I have had to take forgiveness seriously in order to survive spiritually and psychologically.

B. MY BROTHER

My brother, Pete, decided to stop speaking to me over a decade ago, although I would like nothing more than to have a good relationship with him. Unfortunately, due to a long and bitter divorce from Pete's first wife, he has become estranged from his three—now adult—children. If my understanding of our relationship is correct, Pete feels betrayed by me because I continue in relationship to his children and am thus closer to his children than he is. I am closer because I chose not to take sides in his divorce in order to maintain my relationship with Pete's children. I suspect

Pete feels that I betrayed him. Needless to say, the situation is far more complicated than my simplified analysis, and what is most important to you as reader is this—first, Pete felt so alienated by me that he stopped communicating with me, and second, I acted as I did because I felt that placing children ahead of adults was the best approach in a complicated situation.

Having said that, losing my brother has been one of the most painful experiences of my adult life. I need Pete, particularly as we age, and I love him. I love him because I have always loved my siblings and because we are now just three of us remaining, Pete, Nancy and me. We are the only three who share the same childhood experiences and parents, three who can can laugh and cry and talk about the craziness of those early years.

How have I forgiven Pete? I want to be quick to say that I have forgiven him, am forgiving him, and will probably need to forgive him for the rest of my life. It is not done, this spiritual work of mine.

Importantly, I have had to let go of the deep pain I experience by Pete's continued rejection of me. Losing my brother has felt like a death, a loss that I still grieve. Similarly, I have had to let go of any claim I might have on our relationship. No matter what I do to try to "fix" or mend our relationship, it continues to be broken. I have had to come to terms with the fact that I have no control over Pete and his response to me.

Prayer helps; it softens my attitude. And time. Time lubricates my heart.

Which leads to third, I've had to put myself in Pete's shoes, to feel some of the pain he has felt, which as you can imagine has been tremendous, losing all relationship with his children. Pete's life has been hard, which is some of his own doing, but he, like I, was raised in a dysfunctional family. What did that mean to him? I have had to ask that question, though I am not likely to receive answers.

And finally, I've had to ask myself what I could have done differently, where did I fail in our relationship and in how I handled things?

C. BOB W

It took years for me to forgive Maranatha leader Bob W. I worked for the organization for over two years, which meant that Bob was my boss. He was a bully, and although I was among the least bullied on staff, I watched him berate and emotionally bruise other people—people I cared about, people who did not defend or know how to defend themselves. Worse, Bob only knew of and taught about a harsh god—as in, "I knew that you were a harsh man, reaping where you did not sow, and gathering where you did not [sow]. . ." (Matt. 25:24) Bob preached love backed by hell and fire, and I came to resent Bob for trying to bind my soul as tightly as was his bound. (Obviously I take full responsibility for letting that happen to me. I have had to accept my role in acceding to such a negative theology—but that point, my acceptance—leads to an important note about forgiveness. The other person, the one needing our forgiveness, might have done little or nothing wrong. Our perception of their wrong is so often what is at play.)

How did I forgive Bob? Years later, on Facebook, I wrote Bob a note telling him candidly how I felt. To his credit, Bob apologized. Not for his damning theology, which may be as damning and damaging as ever, but for his bullying.

It occurs to me as I write that one reason Bob's bullying was painful for me is that I was bullied when I was twelve years old, something that at the time left me feeling emasculated. I resented that feeling, and looking back, the adult in me understands that I should have spoken-up in the moment when Bob bullied someone. Only, Maranatha (as I've said) was a Christian cult, in essence, and I felt cowed, something I take responsibility for.

D. CHRIST CHURCH

While serving as the rector of Church in Sausalito, 2005–10, I was stalked by one of the parishioners. Despite my efforts to thwart this person, the stalking continued unabated. I needed the help of both the bishop and my vestry (lay leadership), yet both declined to intervene. I left Christ Church following three years of stalking because of the psychological toll the stalking took on me and over concern for my family. When I left Christ Church, the vestry retaliated against me by forcing me and my children out of the church house (rectory), our home of five years, within two weeks, despite several assurances that we would be allowed to take longer to move. Worse, about half of the parishioners—people who had befriended me and I thought cared for me as both a human being and a priest—shunned me. Many of these people have not spoken to me again to this day. I was cursed and gossiped about cruelly and openly for months. I felt as though I had been stoned emotionally.

How did I forgive, or am I forgiving? I had a good therapist who helped me understand the nature of stalking, the response of the parish to my leaving, and the very subtle and temporary PTSD that I likely experienced (according to my therapist). I chose and am still choosing to forgive, though for the most part, this experience has become an historic experience in my life. I also came to understand that those people who shunned me felt as though I had betrayed them by leaving. Many of them did not appreciate or understand the situation regarding the stalking, or (as I was told) they felt as though I should have moved to a church farther away than the seven miles' distance to St. Stephen's, my new parish.

One day near the end of my tenure at Christ Church, I was praying about the situation—being stalked without resolution—when I experienced this epiphany: that God had known all along what would happen—had advance knowledge that I would suffer through Christ Church, with both the stalking and the sense of betrayal—and hard as it all was for me, God was never afraid for me to walk through this *valley of the shadow*. God's faith sustained me when my faith proved to be inadequate. God knows our trials and is never afraid for us.

E. ASCENSION

Christ Church is not the only parish I've had to forgive. A group of parishioners at the Church of the Ascension in Knoxville, where I served for a several years beginning in 2015, decided they wanted me to leave long before time and without cause. These people attacked me viciously, making my life there miserable and my management of the parish untenable. I chose to leave because I was close to retirement and knew that I would not have the fortitude to fight and to make the cure work.

Forgiveness in this instance required me to recognize—again with the help of a good therapist—the role that *shame* played. I was ashamed of the failure, that no matter how hard I tried, I was unable to make the relationship between Ascension (as a whole) and me work. I felt as though I had failed as a priest and as a person. Removing the feeling of shame from my life enabled me to begin the hard work (that continues to this day) of forgiving. I should like to observe as I write that even now I feel energy over the situation, some defensiveness, a hint that I still have some work to do in forgiving Ascension.

F. THE LONG AND WINDING ROAD

These instances in which I've had to work forgiveness are real. As I reread, the descriptions sound clinical to me, but the road towards forgiveness in each instance has been long and winding, painful and emotional. In each of these cases, I've had to examine myself both inside and out, from inside and outside; I've also had to wrestle with the relationships, almost always alone—and by that I mean that the other parties were either unwilling to participate, or simply unavailable. Like I said, forgiveness takes courage, a strength that comes only from grace and time.

Perhaps you remember when Dylann Roof killed nine people at the church in Charleston, South Carolina. A daughter of one of the victims announced solemnly and immediately that she forgave Dylann Roof, because her faith required it of her. I wondered then how she could possibly forgive Roof so quickly. Could I do what she was doing if I found myself in the same situation? Certainly not. A year or two later, I read that this same woman described her forgiveness as a process, that she had not, after all, been able to forgive instantly. Instead, as she described it, forgiveness took or takes time. As in, I choose to forgive, I am working on forgiving, and by God's grace, I will forgive.

Father, forgive me my trespasses as *I forgive others* . . . not *because* I forgive others.

I wonder, then, is God's forgiveness of me a process? Or is God's forgiveness instantaneous? What if my own wrongs are continuous or habitual?

G. END NOTES

It bears repeating, forgiving others does not require reconciliation or that a person continue in a destructive relationship. A battered wife should not return to her brutal husband. An emotionally abused child ought to escape emotional abuse when she comes of age.

Sadly, forgiving others can be isolating and lonely, such as when I left Ascension prematurely. Yet, I think back to Madeline L'Engle's quip, when it comes to the sins of others, should I choose to retain them, whatever will I do with them? Far too many people lash out in retaliation, causing far worse harm to others, just because they have been hurt.

I have written far more about forgiveness than I had intended, and I've not found a way to relay the stories of the tough times in my life without resurrecting some of my own latent feelings of hurt and anger. I have shared real instances from and among real people, not to disparage anyone, but to splay my own spiritual struggles for consideration. Broadly speaking, I am a man at peace, inside and out, but I am also a man carved by relationships, both successful and unsuccessful. These are among my most unsuccessful relationships.

Yet forgiveness of others is at the end of the day, not just psychological, it is spiritual. Failure to engage in the process of forgiveness tends to block grace in one's life. I know because I have experienced blockage.

Someone recently asked me, how could he forgive his son's murderer? (I am relaying this question with permission.) How do you answer such questions? Except with sadness, a heavy heart, and the simple words, *You just have to.* You have to try. And you have to ask God for grace. You don't want to carry that brick of anger forever. You don't want your heart broken forever. You don't want to be a shriveled-up old man with barely a chip of soul remaining. *You just have to.* And as I write these words, a tear of compassion falls from my eye.

Twenty-Six

The Sea Vista, II

THE HAPPIEST TIME OF my childhood was while living at the Sea Vista Motel. I learned to swim in the swimming pool there. Three of the four of us kids—Pete was too young—took lessons from this wonderful couple who would come to the motel and teach us together. They taught us to hold onto the concrete ledge surrounding the pool and kick; once we mastered kicking, they told us to drop our heads face first into the water while kicking and while holding onto the ledge. Eventually we would swim out to one of them standing in the middle of the pool with our heads down, kicking, and finally, they taught us strokes, like the crawl, or breast.

Nancy and I became good little swimmers, so they enrolled us in local children's swim competitions. I still have ribbons from our meets. Water and land became the same to me, so at home did I feel in the water. I would swim and play and float and dive. When friends came over, we would race each other to see who was fastest and who could swim the farthest underwater without taking a breath.

These days, living in the northern Rockies, I watch kids learning to downhill ski. Just like swimming for me, skiing becomes second nature, something that rarely happens when a person waits until adulthood to learn.

I remember Christmases just as fondly from those days, with our 60's Christmas trees decorated with bubble lights. Once we'd placed ornaments on the tree, we'd take handfuls of dime store tinsel and chuck them at the tree. Mom never once reprimanded us or told us to lay the strands on the tree one at a time. Nan, my mother's mother, would drive down from Tennessee loaded with her old Cadillac full of presents. She was Santa Claus and we couldn't wait for her to arrive.

For my birthdays, I would invite school friends over for a party and the Menu Restaurant would bring over a five gallon tub of coffee ice cream. We'd run and play and swim in the pool, slide down the water slide, and eat chocolate cake with that ice cream. To this day, Nancy and I both like coffee ice cream best.

The tension that I later experienced with my father did not start until we moved away from the Sea Vista, after he sold it and started developing The Reef Motel. The Reef was more of a seventies' Florida resort motel, Polynesian style. Maybe it was the stress he faced while building, or maybe he felt starved musically, having no outlet to play his jazz. Maybe turning nine changed me psychologically or physiologically so that I became more aware of family dysfunction. Regardless, my childhood up until I turned nine was pleasant enough, and our days at that quirky aqua motel were sweet. We felt like family.

Twenty-Seven

The Blowing Snow
written in 2008

THE YELLOWS WERE SUN-BRIGHT. The oranges pumpkin, and the reds a deep hue of scarlet. The soft Appalachian mountains glowed the incandescence of Fall. From Lake Logan anchoring the valley, the hills rose as fire lapping gently to the sky, and that is how I found North Carolina in late October, when I arrived Monday morning for CREDO retreat. Monday night, the sky filled with clouds, wispy at first. Ice crystals encircled the moon, something Appalachian folklore says portends snow. It doesn't snow in North Carolina in October, at least not very often, but this October it did.

It snowed, and by morning, a manna frost of white formed lightly on grass, split rails, and mossy stones.

We gathered Tuesday for Morning Prayer in Celebration Hall, the camp's chapel. Enormous windows framed the snow. As I sat in prayer and watched, the snow became a gift that transported me to another place and time—*home*. The snow that by now was blowing felt like home because I remember so many times in Tennessee, whose hills are gentle like the North Carolina mountains, warming myself by a fire, staring outside at falling snow. And here I was, rocking myself by the hearth of soul, watching snow swirl and blow in North Carolina, and I returned home in one of those ways unique to the heart. Home, with the warm solitude of the cold snow.

Returning home reminds me of Christmas. I think now of Christmas, and the infant Jesus who found home among animals, in an old weather-worn barn. Mary held him tightly, committing to memory each detail of the night, and what child is homeless as long as his mother holds him? The warmth of breast, the security of solace soft.

Jesus was at home in a world that would never fully welcome him, but Joseph was not at home that night. Nor was he for many nights to come. He was a Galilean. He found himself in Bethlehem, several days' travel (southward) away from his family. Worse, the angel of the Lord appeared to Joseph without warning—he could not prepare for such an event—and led him further south, still, to Egypt. Joseph *became* the sons of Jacob, exiled in a country not his own, among people not his family, for purposes beyond his dreams and imagination. Contrary to his own life's design, Joseph entered a destiny far greater than anything he had considered, all because an angel of the Lord said, "Go." Perhaps that is where Joseph found home—not in Bethlehem or Egypt or even Galilee, but in that one simple word, "Go."

We gather as family at Christmas to see spiritual snow swirl and fall outside, and if we don't have family nearby, we gather as friends and church people and acquaintances because the act of gathering feels like home to people in exile—the gathering itself becomes the snow blowing around the soul's shadows. We as exiles are taken to homelands distant and remote, across temporal chasms, all by the company of others, and all because we long for something we cannot identify, something we cannot access, something we cannot in the end control. We long for home, we long for that place by the fire

But we are not home in the way we would like; we are a Joseph people in exile. Yet the Christmas promise to a people so far from home is that home is a bare space away. That snow swirls about you in ways and creating depths you did not know. Maybe, just maybe, you like Joseph will find home in a simple word—only your word is different. It can't be *go* for you have gone. Perhaps your word is . . . *kneel*.

Come adore on bended knee,
Christ the Lord, the newborn King.[1]

Kneel in awe at the gentle work of God on this night of new creation. Kneel in awe at the presence of Divinity wearing the clothes of humanity. Kneel in awe at the absolute and perfect love of a God who has, after all this, welcomed you home.

---

1. Chadwick, J. (1862). *Angels we have heard on high* [Traditional carol, adapted from "Les Anges dans nos campagnes"].

Twenty-Eight

Worship the Lord . . . in spirit and in truth . . .

I AM STILL NOT sure what it means for me to be a priest. I mean, I understand what the tradition tells me, that a Christian priest ordained in *Apostolic Succession* is the spiritual offspring of Peter. Hands were laid upon heads across generations, dating each priest to Peter. I also understand Christian priesthood finds its roots in the Levitical priesthood, dating to the second millennium, B.C.E., and that some form of priesthood existed more broadly throughout the ancient near east and in other traditions, places, and times.

Many people consider a priest to be an interlocutor, someone who stands between them and God, who offers prayers on their behalf and listens to God for them. I understand this attribution, which is not to say I agree with it. So I continue to be uncertain about what it means for *me* to *be* a priest. As in, embody priesthood, live the life of a priest, be a person called out as somehow separate or different, viewed with esteem or disdain, treated as a curiosity, the object of projections. What does it mean? Some or all of these things, or none of them at all? And, where does worship come in?

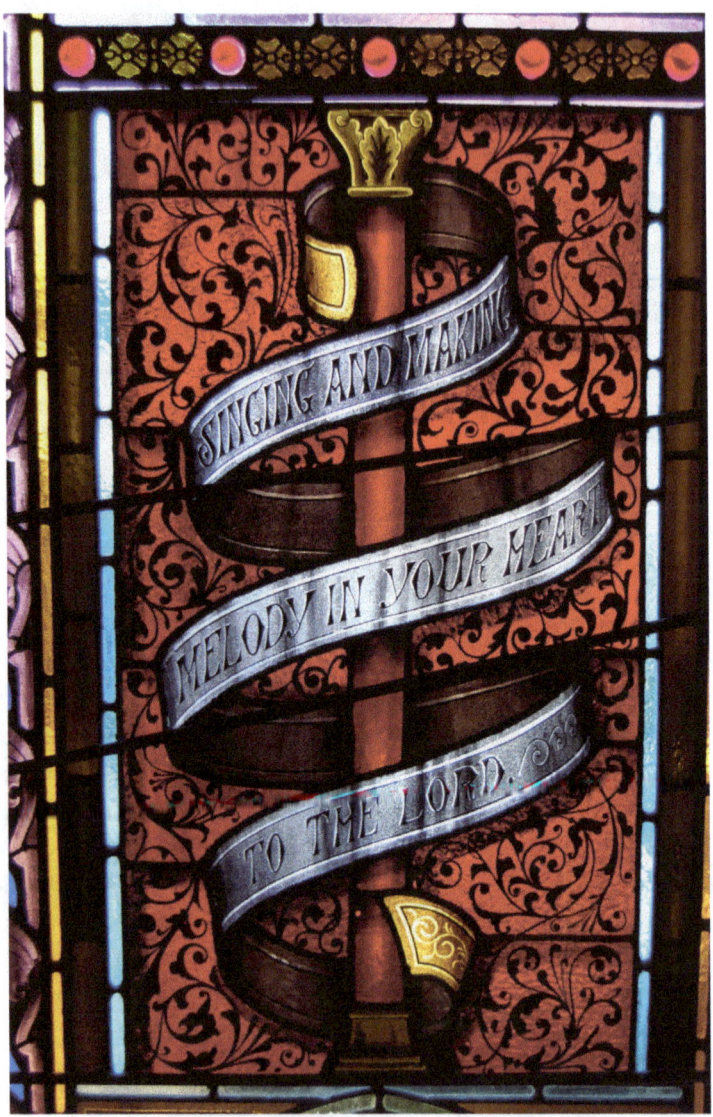

Thinking about Jesus, I cannot recall a single time the Gospels describe his worship or his worshiping. He prayed. He taught his disciples to pray. He went off by himself to a *lonely* place to pray. He prayed in the company of the disciples, at the Last Supper and prior to breaking and multiplying bread and fish, before many miracles, and following his resurrection. But, did he worship? He respected and attended feasts and celebrations, like the wedding at Cana and Passover; as a child, he made pilgrimage to Temple with his parents.

To be sure, I feel certain Jesus *did* worship. After all, he *understood* worship. He taught his disciples the Lord's Prayer, and the prayer begins by worship: *Hallowed be Thy name.* I just cannot recall a passage in the Gospels when he, himself, is recorded as actually worshipping.

Perhaps the closest example of Jesus worshipping might be found his "high priestly prayer," recorded by John and spoken at the Last Supper. The prayer itself conveys a tone of worship, just not words of worship.

All of this leaves me to wonder, how can we know how to worship properly if Jesus did not leave us an example? I suppose one might point to other snippets of Scripture that offer examples of worship, such as the Psalms, which are replete with lines of worship, such as this one: "Bless the Lord, O my soul, and all that is within me bless his holy name." (Ps. 103:1) The Torah includes several lovely canticles of praise and thanksgiving. The Book of Acts, though not transcribing the actual words Paul and Silas used, indicates that they sang hymns to God, love songs.

Forgive me for saying so, but read two dimensionally and without emotion, these examples might not *feel* worshipful, much like some hymns on a Sunday morning can feel more rote than worshipful.

The few stories of worship in Scripture portray it as emotional. There is King Saul in ecstasy like some sort of whirling dervish, spinning about among the prophets of his day. Then there is David, seen dancing and fist pumping, rejoicing and jumping and shouting in front of the ark of covenant, so much so that his wife disdained him in that moment, as embarrassed as an Episcopalian at a Pentecostal service.

Worship, and I have heard priests and theologians define worship as, "ascribing worth to something," such as to God. The definition feels vapid for any number of reasons, starting with this conundrum: is a lowly human being capable of ascribing worth to Divine Mystery? Doesn't worth exist intrinsically within the godhead? It seems to me that we have neither authority nor ability to add worth to God. We might acknowledge worth and even bow down to it, both of which seem far closer to spiritual worship than merely *ascribing worth*. But oughtn't worship consist of something more? Surely it is multifaceted: literal, metaphorical, lyrical, poetic, all-encompassing, from the heart, and self-abandoning.

The most colorful images of worship in the Christian Scriptures are found in the Book of Revelation, with its combination of Disney-esque light-show and Saul-like ecstatic dancing. The problem with Revelation, though, is its violence; the writer condemns the majority of earth's people to an eternal fire in the name of a loving God.

Worship. I picture the Munchkins when the house fell on the wicked witch of the west, canting their gleeful song of joy in parade, to Dorothy:

> "Let's open up and sing, and ring the bells out
> Ding-dong! the merry-o, sing it high, sing it low..."[1]

Psalmists beseech the faithful to praise God in dance. (Ps. 149:3; 150:4) I recently attended a concert hosted by the Canterbury Choir at the Church of the Heavenly Rest in New York City. The concert included Duke Ellington's sacred music and concluded with his piece, "Praise God and Dance." The jazz group performed and soprano Ta'Nika Gibson sang this amazing piece that tracks the psalm with lyrics compelling worshippers to sing and play instruments and then if still not enough, to dance! As they played, the artist Alysia Velez came sweeping through the church in a flowing red gown, dancing gloriously up and down the aisles to Ellington's vivacious music, exfoliating worship with each movement, representing union of the human soul with the force

---

1. Lyrics from "Ding-Dong! The Witch Is Dead," written by Harold Arlen (music) and E.Y. Harburg (lyrics), from *The Wizard of Oz* (1939). © EMI Feist Catalog Inc. Used under fair use.

behind all of life! How can one not dance, at the least in our souls, at the realization of the enormity of grace behind Love?

All this leads back to the priesthood and church, or so it seems to me. We come to church to worship, and I'm not sure we do it particularly well. Think of the Resurrection, a house has fallen hard on the wicked witch, evil and death. Death has been destroyed and evil's days are now numbered. *Ding-dong the witch is dead.* God has done this. And, whatever you believe about Easter morning, surely it is something to dance about? To shout and clap and sing? No dirges allowed.

However Jesus himself worshipped, and I suspect he did, what I also suspect is this. Jesus viewed God (as Father or as whatever honorific or attribution you'd like to apply) as absolutely, completely, and enthrallingly joyous. *Sing it high, sing it low . . .*

To see clarity in one's soul the height and depth and to witness the love and kindness of the Eternal—to see it as one sees the Teton's or Australia's Great Barrier Reef and the hues darting about in the guise of fish, colors you wonder might not exist anyplace else on earth? *Ding dong . . .* Oh, my goodness. How can one not fall down in complete silence, or jump up and down in absolute ecstasy, at the awe-some presence of that which is Divine?

The Great *I am,* The I am that I am, The I will be what I will be . . . and for the flash of an instant you get the briefest glimpse of something eternal . . .

> *The Lord is in their holy Temple; Let all the earth keep silence before them.*

Fall. To. The. Ground. In. Silence.

And for all the things a parish wants its priest to do—lead services, counsel parishioners, organize social justice, preach erudite sermons, balance budgets, manage employees, maintain a building, be socially lovely, wear the right clothes—*for all the things,* I have come to conclude that the most important item is not on anyone's list.

Worship. God. In. The. Beauty. Of. Wholeness.

Love the Lord your God with all your heart, with all your soul, and with all your mind. Then you are free to love your neighbor, and please love that neighbor as you love yourself.

Oh, my God. Love God—and while I am still not entirely sure what it means for me to be a priest, the one thing I can do and want to do and hope to do is this: Love the Lord my God.

The erotic Song of Songs removes love for God from stilted, two-dimensional worship and throws it headlong into a four-dimensional life. That night five decades ago when I knelt beside Mom and she prayed for me to receive the Holy Spirit, I felt joy. I felt ecstasy. I felt worship—not because I understood—I didn't—any single piece of what I was uttering, but because I gave myself over to the Divine from deep within my heart. To something the late Catherine Marshall dubbed, *Beyond Our Selves,* the title to her book on the engagement of faith and the Holy Spirit, or in my case, *beyond myself.*

Later, from church Faith Alive's, I learned simple songs that connected me emotionally, and in Maranatha—with all its faults—we would lift our hands in a worship that felt vibrant. Next to my own bed at night as a teenager, I would sing simple songs that would allow me to give myself over, and when that would happen, I would whisper words of prayer in sync with the compassion I felt from God. My deepest prayer always seems to start with worship.

As a seminarian, I learned silence, and silence just like these other methods (for that is what they are, methods) stilled my soul enough to give myself over to that which is *beyond ourselves.* In each of these ways, I felt communal with the Eternal, somewhere below emotions, and when that happens, I find that I am able to pray for important things in my world, most often individuals, with a type of spiritual sincerity and integrity, an outgrowth of communion with God. I felt I was praying what God was praying, I feel that I am praying for whom Jesus is praying.

Church hymnody and the Eucharist sometimes feel—though not always—two dimensional, particularly when done just to get done, or done without emotion. Most composers and authors likely intended their hymns to do what I am describing, guide a congregation to a different place, into connection. The same could be said of the Eucharist, as a sacrament, intended to connect people to spiritual grace. Yet, many hymns feel flat and the Eucharistic prayer rote.

Although I am not entirely sure what it means to be a priest, I am sure of one thing, that my call is the same call as to every other person on the earth: to worship, to connect with the force giving life behind all of life, the One, the I am, the I will be who I will be. As Jesus said, "The father and I are one." (Jn. 10:30) And, his prayer for us was to be the same. One.

Twenty-Nine

Sex and Sexuality

From every family, language, people, and nation,
a kingdom of priests to serve our God.

And so, to him who sits upon the throne,
and to Christ the lamb,
Be worship and praise, dominion and splendor,
for ever and for evermore.

—BCP, p. 94 (quoting Rev. 5: 10, 13)

THE SONG OF SONGS reminds us how important sex is to both faith and humanity. Curiously, the Bible does not treat sex as taboo the way so many people of faith do or think it does. Jesus never spoke against sex, except to hint that sexual infidelity is a basis for divorce, and even his one comment seems intended to address the relationship of marriage rather than sex itself. Sexual fidelity is critical to a healthy marriage.

Jesus refused to condemn the woman caught in adultery and he welcomed prostitutes, neither sanctioning nor condemning the behavior of either. Who among you has not sinned? he asked those with rocks in their hands. Worse sins, and strangely enough, I cannot recall Jesus categorizing either premarital sex nor homosexuality as sin, or condemning either.

As far as the Ten Commandments are concerned, only one of them addresses sexual behavior directly, "Do not Commit adultery," and again the commandment has more to do with marital fidelity than it does with sex itself. The last of the Ten Commandments seems to address a person's sexual thoughts, albeit indirectly: "Do not covet your neighbor's wife." The "wife" is listed alongside types of owned property, such as an ox or a donkey, or "anything that belongs to your neighbor." In other words, the commandment appears to treat women as property, and is about neither sex nor sexuality.

I am wary of being too dismissive of Scripture with regard to sex, as sex and sexuality go to the heart of faith and the person. Plus, among the 613 laws of Moses, any number of them criminalize certain sexual behaviors. Generally, both our modern society and our faith communities ignore these prohibitions and their potent punishments. I cannot, for example, recall a single time someone I know watched from the sidelines while a town stoned his daughter for falsely presenting herself as virgin. I do not believe I have ever witnessed a couple legally killed because of their adultery.

Paul addressed sexual matters more frequently than Jesus did, mostly from what seems like a negative view of sex and sexuality. He decried marriage as a weaker state, as though sexual impulses might sully a person and her faith. He made negative references to a form of homosexuality, although we cannot know exactly what he meant.[1] He condemned fornication.

Over the years, the church has seen fit to temper Paul in much the same way that Paul and the early church tempered the traditions they inherited. For example, Paul and the early church eschewed the ages-old requirement of circumcision, and they admitted non-Jews into the Christian-Jewish church. Today, I do not know anybody

---

1. Paul it is believed was condemning the practice of Roman soldiers taking young (underage) boys as their sex slaves.

who thinks women should remain silent in church or cover their heads as a symbol of submissiveness to their husbands.

 I do not mean to sound argumentative, nor will I wade deeper into the Scriptural morass regarding sex and sexuality than I already have. I am certainly not a Bible scholar, and there are many who have written eloquently on this topic.

Instead, I would simply say this: sex is a beautiful and lovely way for two people to unite their love, both physically and spiritually. Their expression of love becomes a safe harbor, a way to hold and protect each other from the dangerous seas of a challenging world. Isn't such love a gift from God? Even the myth of creation relates the idea that God gave Eve and Adam to each other for companionship, physical and otherwise. Moreover, the sex drive is innate, God-given, and that not just for humans, but for almost all of the animal world. Earth-natural, so I have to wonder at faiths—not just Christianity, but others, also—that regard sex and sexuality as dirty and disdainful, that limit it to procreation. Rather than a communion to be celebrated with great joy.

Of course, the line is thin between healthy and unhealthy sexual activity, between mutuality and compulsion. Psyches can be so easily damaged, particularly when trust is violated, or when one person forces themselves on another. People become vulnerable during voluntary sex, meaning that sex can be used manipulatively in relationships. There ought to be and is a morality regarding sexual behavior, although I hear people claim that sexual morality is an individual matter. Perhaps, although it seems that the sense and action of love proffers basic and obvious guidelines—the treating of the other as more important than oneself. Like with Scriptural interpretation, I leave morality up to moral theologians and moral philosophers, but other than coerced sex (rape, slave trading, etc.), I have a hard time imagining any act of sex, misdeeds included, requiring punishment or prison. Likewise, I have a hard time picturing God sending people to a fiery hell of eternal punishment because of their sexual behavior or misbehavior. In short, I suspect that God is not as wigged-out about sex as we are.

I was at one point in my life, wigged-out about sex. I suppose the reasons for this are both complex and simple.

Complex because one's sexuality is typically complex, genetically and psychologically, spiritually and physically. For me, as a bisexual person, this has proved to be especially so. The world in which we live—even where more progressive than regressive—typically requires people to choose. Which are you, straight or gay?

Heterosexual or homosexual? You cannot be both. I have had prospective suitors reject me outright because they think I am lying to them and myself when I claim to be bisexual. I disagree.

Years ago, Alfred Kinsey developed a sliding scale regarding sexuality, something that feels accurate. At one end of the scale is heterosexuality and at the other end is homosexuality, with most people falling somewhere along the scale, being some mix of both. I find myself near the middle. I understand and appreciate that there are some people who are clearly either/or, and not both, but that is not me. Each person gets to identify ourselves for ourselves. What that means for me is this: returning to my teenage prayer. "God make me honest with you, and honest with myself."

Simple, because in my family, nobody talked about sex. Nobody, even to this day talked or talks about sex. When I faced puberty, my mother slipped me a little book entitled something like, "Sixty Questions to Ask the Stork." Fortunately for me, the questions came with answers, as none of my teachers and nobody at church ever talked about sex. Conversations about sex in my world was limited to pubescent boys telling jokes and sharing dark stories.

How do people—our children—learn about sex if we as a people continue in our repression? If I could now instruct my very young parents back in the day, I would tell them to kiss each other more often and more passionately, in front of us children, to hold hands, to tease, to be naturally in love. I would urge them to teach us through conversation and by their mutual respect in both their love and arguments, including in how they would make-up after arguing. And when the time was to come, which it did, I would have wanted them to teach me a few of the basics—and to encourage questions whenever or however I'd have liked. I certainly had more than a few questions.

I suspect that Mom must have known that I harbored feelings for men, not just women, only her religious rigidity made her fear for me. My best friend in college—Joe—was gay. He was also three years older than I was, and when I told my mother about Joe as my friend (not about his being gay), even before she met him, she was—I could tell—apprehensive, even suspicious. Why would a guy three years older befriend her son? I suppose she thought he might corrupt me, or worse, bring out the latent side of me she already suspected was there. Mom certainly sent subliminal messages to me that being gay would be unacceptable and wrong. She later articulated this prejudice using religious terms, that anything but married sex is unacceptable to God.

It took me years to become comfortable with my sexuality, and even more years to be willing to date men. The freedom to become myself proved to be one of the last—and perhaps most important—steps to my becoming more fully myself. More human. Which brings to mind the baptismal covenant in the Episcopal Church, calling on each of us to, "respect the dignity of every human being." (BCP 305) There is dignity in being sexually honest.

And isn't that what each of us wants, and isn't what God dreams for each of us? That we can in freedom and humility become more truly ourselves, to live on the outside more honestly who we discover ourselves to be on the inside?

When I "came out" regarding my bisexuality, I told only those people who needed to know—those people who are close to me and who share my life in a personal way: my kids, other family members, close friends, and some people in church. I felt no need to tell everyone in the world, nor do I to this day. I do not know of any straight person who says upon meeting a stranger, "Hi, I'm Rob and I am straight."[2]

You see, one's sexuality need not be secret, but for me, I hold it as private.

---

2. It is worth noting the Harvey Milk argument that by coming out of the closet to everyone, the gay community would (and did) normalize being gay. In fact, being "openly" gay by so many people has been important to the broader society.

Thirty

Shells

I wrote this piece for the April 26, 2023 edition of Episcopal Journal, Speaking to the Soul.

"I learned solitude walking on the beach. The cascade and cadence of waves, their repetition gaping and crashing, gaping and crashing, endlessly rolling to shore, I would walk alone with my thoughts and angst and dreams. And I would sometimes wonder where you are, O Lord, even as I might wonder at your presence. Like Jesus with the disciples at the shore, a filament of presence.

I would also hunt for shells. Perfect shells, cowries and olives and scallops. Sand dollars, too, whole ones that would make me feel dollar-richer with each find. It wasn't until I entered middle age—still a beachcomber—that I noticed the beauty of broken shells. Half shells, shells sanded by time and tide. Conglomerates, too, shells mortared one against another against another. A friend once heard me mention shells in this way and gave me a conglomerate of oyster shells for my desk, as a reminder that we, too, are beautifully imperfect.

As a reminder that our better selves have been sanded by time and tide. Beautiful shells, those allowing the complexities of life to buffer, temper, and deepen them.

Solitude, spending forty days alone with both thoughts and demons taught Jesus what is important in life, by the negative. Not wealth nor power nor even religious fervor. No, these are not what connect a human to God and others. It is something else, something longing to emerge from deep within, though so often stifled by wealth and power and religious fervor.

Do you know what makes people happiest? Fulfilled? Relationships, of course. Connection. One to another, and one to one's

God. Studies and intuition and even Jesus' command to love prove this to be true.

So I wonder, also as part of my walking in solitude, do we seek these other things?

Rather than love?

Thirty-One

Behind the Veil

HANDS IN THE DIRT. I touch the heart of God when I dig in the garden. When I hike alone, through the mountains with my dogs. Solitude. When I exert myself physically, and when I lose myself to the piano. Yes, and sometimes when I pray, though not always when I pray, and yes, sometimes when I read, though not always when I read. When I throw an intimate dinner party, and Spirit flits in and among the words spoken, and those unspoken. And always when I paint.

So many people have written about God in nature that I need not repeat what they have said. Suffice it to say, being in nature in solitude is retreat and restoration. *Feeling* being alive.

Several years ago, I walked Camino de Santiago through Spain. "The Way," Camino is a pilgrim's trek most typically launched in the Pyrenees east at St. John Pied de Port, France, and finished at the Cathedral of St. James in Santiago de Compostela. "Santiago" means *St. James,* and the route is believed to be the route over which St. James' followers carried his bones to Santiago.

I encountered all types of weather conditions walking Camino from March into April: sun, rain, hail, snow, fog, warmth, cold, wind and dead calm. Regardless of each day's weather, I would be outside, walking. Still closer to God than I would have been had I stayed indoors.

One day, the rain pelted hard against me. I leant into the wind, my rain gear barely keeping me dry and my boots barely anchoring me. This Camino path stretched along a slant of spring hillside, trees atop, profiled skeleton black against the still-winter sky. I closed my eyes, and I swear I felt myself lift like a kite off the ground.

Like dreams I've had. Without wings, without aircraft, arms stretched upward, almost like Superman, only wider apart. It has been several years since I dreamt of flying, though dreams aloft are my favorite. Spirit as wind lifts me into the air where I whisk about freeform, and that is what I felt as I walked along with the wind and rain pushing hard against me. So very so very alive. Mystically alive.

I am not a mystic, though I believe in mysticism. I believe in spiritual connection, in things both seen and unseen. I believe in mysticism because of the testimony of others. Because of St. John and his stories, because of the dozens of people over the years who have shared with me their mystical experiences. I believe in a space beyond the pale into which we cannot gaze, absent imagination and grace.

Laura my wife died in June of 2002 from a combination of gallbladder surgery, a cruel pain disease, and a body weakened by pain, medicine, and hunger. She wasn't able to eat for the two weeks leading up to surgery. Tate was seven years old and Tilly was four. Laura wanted them to experience DisneyWorld, so we took them in May of that year. She experienced such a severe gallstone attack that she was hospitalized and her doctor told her he would not release her until she had surgery. She—we—decided to return to Maryland for the surgery so I could manage the kids better at home. She had the surgery two long weeks later and died following that surgery, weakened from pain and hunger.

During Laura's time in the surgical recovery room, prior to her discharge and death, my friend Don Rypka stayed with me in an empty hospital waiting room. Afternoon light was slipping into night darkness when suddenly the skies outside grew black. Lightning flashed and thundered. Centuries-old trees swayed fiercely to the flashes of ethereal light, and I swear I felt the ground quake. The storm blew through as an omen I ignored. I took Laura home anyway, home to die, despite the omen.

As I've written elsewhere, still in the car before entering the hospital, she asked me to bless her—to be a priest. This was the only time I ever acted as her priest, something we'd agreed upon years earlier. I was her husband. Her lover. Her companion. Not her priest.

"The Lord bless you and keep you; the Lord make his face to shine upon you and be gracious unto you. The Lord lift up his countenance upon you, and give you peace. Now and forever." I prayed, marking her forehead with the sign of the cross. The same cross painted with dirt on your forehead on Ash Wednesday, "...you are dust, and to dust you shall return." (BCP 265) The same mark made with chrism oil at baptism, "You . . . are marked as Christ's own forever." (BCP 308)

I blessed her and she died.

I have dreamt of Laura any number of times in the scores of years since then, that June 7. Only once have I experienced the

Laura in my dream *as* Laura. I cannot even describe the dream to you, except to say that the presence was real. It was her.

Mystically.

And these years later, I do not recall any specific message conveyed in that dream, whether she was trying to tell me she was okay or whether she was trying to tell me anything at all. I doubt it, as I had never wondered whether she was okay, now beyond the veil. I do, however, vaguely recall the dream carrying some attendant sense of assurance, though of what I cannot say. Maybe joy more than assurance. But, and I suppose this is my point, her presence was real enough to assuage any doubts I might have had regarding the mystical, the beyond the veil. The amount of reality, of substance, that hides just behind the pale.

Years ago I started thinking differently of eternity, as not just a physical, one place gilded called heaven, and another place painful and punishing called hell. As an aside, I now consider any "hell" that might exist as being the absence of life. If I'm right, then some death would be just that for some people, death.

As to heaven, heaven is life. Perhaps a physical place, too. Certainly a place different from here. In my mind heaven falls into the physicists' modern concept of multiple dimensions existing side by side. When a person dies, the partition separating this imperfect or infected dimension or universe from the more perfect one next door opens in some minuscule way, say like a pinprick, and the soul is pulled from this dimension into that one. Where there is no defect, where there is love. And faith. And hope. The streets are paved with love, faith and hope. Gold.

The witnesses of so many people across the years have reinforced my experience of Laura coming to me in a dream. Like I said, I did not need the dream to make myself feel better nor to assuage my grief. I handled grief as well as anyone might, to the extent of course that grief can be handled or controlled—with some grace and the love of family and friends. No, I did not need the dream to heal my broken heart. Thinking now about it, perhaps, just perhaps, the dream was connected to the blessing I'd given Laura. Maybe blessings are real, and terribly, terribly important.

I think that about blessings, that they connect us, but who knows whether that explains the significance of the dream? Maybe the dream was nothing more than gift. A simple gift from Laura and the Divine. Mystical.

So you see, when I talk about placing my hands in dirt and feeling the heart of God, I mean it. When I mention painting or playing the piano as physical ways in which I experience this thing called grace, I mean it. These experiences are real, and something unseen happens in the realm in which I see physically, only it is not the painting nor the sound of the music, but the—well, the connection. I feel the heart of God. I pass through, somehow, the veil that was torn in two so long ago, at Jesus' death, from top to bottom.

Thirty-Two

Projections and God

As a priest, I am used to people projecting their view of who and what a priest is or ought to be onto me. People expect me to be what they need me to be, or perhaps they expect me to act and think like they do, or imagine that I am the embodiment of their childhood understanding of a holy person, typically someone set apart. Different. Some people dismiss me, assuming either religion—and therefore a priest—is irrelevant at best, or a person who believes in fairy tales and magic, at worst.

Some projections can be useful. We all try understand of the world around us, and projections help a person do just that. We assume others think or act like we do, or as we think they should. On the other hand, projections can ensnare a person in a web of self-denial and obfuscation. This happens when we become overly comfortable with our version of the world around us, particularly when that version is challenged. Truth is the goal, not one's creation of truth, not truth by projection. Some sort of intellectual and emotional integrity rather than delusion about life, oneself, or others.

Make me honest with you, O Lord, and honest with myself. I've already written about how I started praying that simple prayer when I was a teenager, though who knows why? Perhaps I wanted to know the truth about addiction. I learned early on that people often lie in order to avoid the painful truth about themselves and the damage they unwittingly inflict on others. I did not want to be like my father, and truth—perhaps—would be the best way to avoid that possibility.

It isn't as though I've always been truthful with myself. I certainly did not realize when I started praying the "honesty prayer" that actually becoming honest would be a lifelong project. Without going into all the ways in which I've misled myself over the years, including spiritually, perhaps the greatest has had to do with my sexuality. A person's sexuality goes to their core essence, meaning that being honest about one's sexuality is crucial to emotional, spiritual, and psychological integrity and growth.

I've already written about my lack of sex education as a teen, a problem compounded by my early and immature faith. Being "Christian" when I grew-up meant that any sexual expression outside of marriage was against God's "will." Paul's writing further confused the matter, though I now realize that he, too, was raised, converted and molded in and by his own milieu—his particular cultural and religious setting. Suffice it to say that a "plain reading" of Paul's letters would lead anybody with a conscience to conclude that God does not condone most sexual identities or activities, certainly those that fall outside of either normative[1] or marriage, including sexual identities like mine.

Once I came to terms with my bisexuality, there still remained a shard of dishonesty within me regarding that sexuality. Yes, I knew who I was as a sexual person, but I was afraid to live into that person. I refused to consider dating a man, something a therapist once suggested I do. I quit going to her because the suggestion disturbed me. Perhaps you might wonder why I now think that she was correct, that dating men was necessary for me to be more truly honest with myself. After all, I am *bi*-sexual, which is the rationale I used. I was happy dating women, and dating women was consistent with being who I am as a bisexual person, or so I thought. Only, it wasn't honest. There remained a closeted-ness to me in my unwillingness to date men.

Behind my reticence stood this fact: I was comfortable telling others that God is *not* angry at them because of their sexuality, expressed or otherwise, something I believed about myself, at least intellectually. Yet, there was a functional dishonesty to my life. I was trying to control not only my sexuality, but my relationship with God. As long as I lived on the heterosexual side of myself, I did not have to engage functional faith, just theoretical faith. I could be bisexual, but so what? My behavior was heterosexual. The world considered me to be heterosexual.

Do I trust God enough to be who I am, or not?

My faith was limited and partially false. God loved me—still—as long as I *did* what other people thought was correct for me. I accepted peoples' projections about myself, about my implied sexuality, mostly because I'd encouraged their projections.

---

1. "Norm" in the moral theological sense simply means that which is accepted as applicable to the majority of people, not that a "norm" is the only or correct or moral way for a person to live.

PROJECTIONS AND GOD

Projections. I have always disliked "clericals"—the clergy black shirt and plastic white collar. Part of the reason I dislike clericals is unique to me. I do not like to stand out or be obvious to others. Wearing clericals marks a person and invites projections. Knowing I am a priest gives people the opportunity to interpret me as priest in ways that I might find unacceptable. Indeed, I believe that we are all "priests" to God, and each of us is responsible for our own spirituality. Each of us has a unique relationship to God, defined by grace and our own leaning into that grace, or not. I do not stand in the place of another. And, in that regard, I need not stand out.

People also project their understanding and expectations of God upon God. I did that—we all do. In my case, I projected my deeply ingrained extraneous religious viewpoints on God, the ones I grew-up with both in my family and as told to me by others. By doing so, I treated God as others treated me—by accepting a false notion of God, a God who could not accept me as I was or am.

I denied God the autonomy of *personhood*. God is *person*, though most of us do not treat God as person. We imagine God to be inflexible, even-tempered, an almost two-dimensional character.

Many Scripture stories reinforce these projections. Just as often, however, Scripture reveals a very different nature regarding God, very person-like. The prophets knew God to express a variety of contrary traits, from anger to judgment to frustration to forgiving to relenting to changing to passionate to jealous to lonely to pleading to compassionate to indomitable.

Who are you, O God, and who am I?

When God told Abraham his plan to destroy Sodom and Gomorrah (a story that is more about hospitality and violence than it is about sexual misbehavior), Abraham negotiated with God. *What if there are forty righteous people? Twenty? Ten?* God proved to be malleable and lowered the standard. Abraham, though, stopped bargaining too soon. I wonder what might have happened had Abraham gone the distance, and reminded God of perfect compassion for imperfect people?

Look what God did for Ninevah, that great city, when Jonah preached to its people? Changed her mind. Or, had God had already forgiven Ninevah, prior to repentance, and sent Jonah to Ninevah just so Nineveh would acknowledge God's grace?

Didn't Jesus teach us to forgive others prior to their repentance? A trait of the Holy that most Christians like to ignore. We think that the *work* of repentance is required, ironically, for salvation, and in thinking that way, we unknowingly project our version of God onto God. Are these projections accurate? What other traits do we project? These days I consider God to be amazingly broad, far more so than I once did. Has God changed, or have I?

J.B.Phillips addressed projections regarding God elegantly in his classic volume, *Your God is too Small*. This book saved me from evangelical fundamentalism more than any other work. *My* God was way too small in those youthful days of evangelical literalism, and no doubt is still too small, for God is indeed great. God is Good. Greater and better than I can conceive. Eternal and perfect love do not fit into my finite brain.

Thirty-Three

A Habit of Prayer

It occurs to me that it might be helpful to share my habit of prayer—where I typically pray, and how I connect.

Early morning. I spend the first hour of most days at prayer and prayerful reading. I adopted this devotional time during mid-adulthood, about the time I enrolled in seminary at thirty-seven years old.

In seminary, I learned the value of the Morning Prayer service found in the Episcopal Prayer Book, and began using that service as a template for my devotions, meaning I use it neither literally nor completely. Other days, I use the simple outline of a prayer from *The St. Francis Prayer Book*, a gift I received at ordination. Again, I do not follow this prayer structure *religiously*, any more than I do that of the service of Morning Prayer.

Following these templates, I open most mornings with quiet praise. Morning Prayer inaugurates with invitation to God: "Lord, open our lips," and the response, "And our mouth shall proclaim your praise," (BCP 80), suggests this: if God opens our mouths, we can do nothing but praise.

Translated: I stand in awe at the Divine power that has brought me to this morning, awake and alive.

I continue with the *Venite* or *Jubilate,* followed by a psalm and readings from some sort of *Scripture.* Scripture to me includes the *Bible,* but often some spiritually-related book, one that will draw me into that prayer space of imagination and release. I have used Thomas Merton and Henri Nouwen and even Alan Watts (Buddhist). Most recently, as you can tell because of quotes from his work, I have read John O'Donohue's *Four Elements.* God and

Spirit and life emerge from between the words of both the Bible and these auxiliary writings.

But, something more than brain work is required to connect with God. John O'Donohue writes about the imagination that is required for people to enter into space with God.[1] By reading a variety of spiritual works, I join with other people in the spaces they have occupied with God. The point is to still my soul each morning and to open myself to God and the universe.

Once I finish reading, I return to the Prayer Book (or the prayers of St. Francis) to continue Morning Prayer, although just as often I let my soul slip into a silence, to *sit* with God. On those days, words feel intrusive, and I set them aside, returning to them when they seem to flow naturally from the stillness.

I write all of this as though it is a perfect exercise, but of course it is not. Many days I have things on my mind or am wrestling with some internal or external conflict—or simply do not have time. The point is not whether or not the time goes well, which is why I remind myself that the control is not mine anyway, certainly not in prayer. The goal is release, to open myself, to let God in my life be God in my life. To let Mystery be Mystery. To let Spirit blow as the wind through the breaches in my soul.

A note about fear. Fear—perhaps this is more so with me than with you—has been a dominant negative emotion in my life, certainly so in my younger years. I find, though, that as I practice faith regularly—most mornings—as I rely increasingly on grace—that fear loses its purchase. As the love of God grows, expands, fills my soul, fear finds fewer and smaller chasms within which to lurk.

Let me also note this. As I have struggled with the major obstacles in my life, for example at Ascension when I felt under personal attack, or at Christ Church when being stalked, I have survived only by the combination of prayer and forgiveness.

Which is why this canticle from Morning Prayer has become so important to me: "Surely it is God who saves me; I will trust in

---

1. O'Donohue, John. Four Elements: Reflections on Nature. London: Bantam Press, 2010, p. 42.

him and not be afraid. For the Lord is my stronghold and my sure defense, and he will be my Savior." (BCP 86)

The apostle encouraged, "Pray without ceasing," (1 Thess. 5:17), which of course is nigh unto impossible when thinking in terms of time and attention. Life is busy and who has the time, much less the energy or spiritual grace to pray constantly? I wonder, though, whether he intended something altogether different, such as an attitude of prayer? A simple trust in a life and world hidden behind the pale, that love is after all directed towards us, and we can in turn direct that love outside ourselves. To love, to put on love, as clothing, to don ourselves in prayer that way? Which means, obviously, that prayer is—again—far more than words.

Thirty-Four

God, Past Present Future

WHO AM I? *O God, and who are you?* If God is one hundred percent inside each atom, each Higgs Boson, completely within each elemental element, and yet, completely without, ubiquitous in a way that even the air is not, I wonder, what of time? What of time that St. Augustine considered to be an element of creation? That God stands out and above time, or distinct from and not bound by time? It boggles my mind to imagine a universe without time. Is that even possible? Is time simply a measure, does it even exist?

And yet, the past, present and future, seem to converge within each of us, as though we—perhaps like God—are repositories of time. Only, my past varies from yours, as do my experiences of the present and the future. You and I might as well live in different dimensions, so divergent are the experiences of our lives.

Each person contains all three within them, don't they? The past, present and future, yet some people choose to live mostly in the past, while others choose to live in the future. Memories bring the past to the present whilst hope advances the future to the present. Today, though, is simply today.

We are asked to live today. Only today.

Esoteric, I suppose, but the question is always the same: I have today, so what will I do with it? From the soul inside to the world outside? Live for good and God and others, and if not that, then what?

Every moment is gift, every breath is one more than I earned, one more than I somehow deserve. I did not ask to be born and by some miracle I am sitting here taking my next unearned breath. In and out, in and out, and the air molecules pulled into my lungs, spirited by lungs to heart, and pumped by heart through blood to the farthest nerve endings. Each molecule contains one hundred percent of God. God lives completely inside each molecule. Every moment, every breath, and God is within and God is without.

More, God is before time and God is beyond time and time itself is merely framework after all, just framework, with God before and God after and God here, here and now.

Who are you, O God? And, who am I, that you choose to live so fully and to be so present within me, in this moment?

Thirty-Five

Prayer

I WROTE EARLIER ABOUT worship and how losing myself to worship leads me into some ethereal room of prayer. The obverse happens, as well, that prayer or words can lead to worship. But remember, rote words are not the same as prayer. Just because words sound like prayer does not make them prayer. Prayer, to borrow from John O'Donohue, is not cerebral; it is ultimately not an activity of the brain.[1] He writes, "Prayer has to do with breathing.... Prayer makes a clearance.... Prayer allows God to be God."[2]

Who are you, O God, and who am I? And how do we learn who God is, this God who lives both within and without, both in this dimension—so hidden—and in the dimension next door, except by translation? Translation from this physical known world into the spiritual world of spirit.

---

1. O'Donohue, p. 17.
2. I don't mean to suggest that rote repetition cannot be prayer, or that words are not important, for reasons I need not explain here. But, my goal is to get us thinking about our relationship with God as something deeper, something at our core, and to encourage us to operate accordingly.

"God is spirit," John wrote, (Jn. 4:24), but then, what is spirit? The Holy Spirit, of course, though any conceptual definition of the Holy Spirit will by nature be incorrect and inadequate. God as Spirit is eternal, and, as sung about Maria in the Sound of Music, "How do you catch a cloud and pin it down?"[3] The wind blows

---

3. Richard Rodgers and Oscar Hammerstein II, *Maria*, in *The Sound of Music*, 1959.

here and there; you recognize it by the movement of trees, or the ripple across water, or the way in which it cools your skin.

Prayer too is wind.

Jesus taught us to begin by acknowledging the tender nature of God as loving parent. *Father,* and not just my father (as I've written elsewhere), but "Our Father,"[4] spoken tenderly, even joyfully, and certainly trustingly. As children.

None of us owns or possesses the nature or person of God, and none of us can apprehend God except with and among others. By that I do not necessarily mean in the presence of others, but with the appreciation that we are all in this together. We are a body of Christ, a body of humanity, each of us a living cell, part of the whole. This concept of communal ownership is expressed throughout the Lord's Prayer, as we invite God's kingdom into our world by shared bread, the generosity of forgiveness, and resistance to evil.

Without invitation of Spirit and spirit, prayer runs the risk of remaining cerebral. But remember, invitation comes to the seeker. The one who seeks finds and the one who asks receives. But how does a person move prayer from the head down to the heart, from the brain to the soul, from the body to God? By knowing the answer to Jesus question: do you not know that *your Father in heaven cares for you more than these?*

Cares for you, and you can settle into and rest in that place of care and abandon as your prayer becomes a giving of yourself over. You abandon yourself, your body, your emotions, your concerns, and *trust* in the Divine Mystery that holds you tenderly, but securely.

In centering prayer, the activity of breathing merges with word to accomplish prayer. Repetition of one's chosen mantra births spiritual rest, moves a person from head to heart. My attempts at a morning ritual with Scripture and prayer/silence is to avail myself of the same spiritual rest. In and out, in and out, and

---

4. I understand how the use of "Father" moves some people into a male dominated patriarchy, but I am content to use the term regardless, knowing that our understanding of God is neither male nor female.

prayer is that settling-in during which you simply *let go.* You simply free God to be God, within and without.

Who are you, O God, and Who am I? I wonder whether it is possible to find out who I am outside of God, or God outside of myself? Prayer, then, must be a knowing. It is a knowing like a husband knows a wife or any combination of intimate partners comes to know the Other.

I mentioned the apostle's words earlier: "Pray without ceasing." (1 Thes. 5:17) I had a friend who tried to do that once, pray without ceasing, only his prayer was cerebral. The guidance he sought by praying was cerebral. Jesus leads in a gentler way, *abide in my love,* as though prayer itself is love, or love is prayer. Walk in love? Live in love. Love is prayer and prayer is love and we know what love is. Abide in means to live in, make your home there. In love.

To not demand our own way. To not notice when others do it wrong. To be patient and kind, to avoid the domination of ego. Love the Lord your God, Love your neighbor, Love Love Love.

Love, they say, casts out fear, and prayer moves a person to bask in the love of God, resting and making one's home there, fear dissipates, dissolves, loses its purchase. There is no fear in the presence of God save for the fear of God, which is a fear altogether different from being afraid. A deep reverence, the farthest understanding or settling in the soul that God is above all and in all and all-encompassing, that God is good after all, all the time, God is good. And therefore, so impossibly are you. Made good by Spirit? Born good? By the cross of Christ good? Simply created good? I cannot say, for those are theological concepts about humanity, but I know that at the end of creation, once God had exhaled *breath,* they declared, *It is Good.*

Good, God is good, the earth is good, and you are improbably yet believably good, by this atomic element we call grace.

Grace.

Thirty-Six

What does the Lord Ordaineth?

REMINISCING ABOUT THE HEBREW patriarch Joseph and his struggles in Egypt, the psalmist wrote something along the lines of, "God sent the Word to test him . . ."

A perennial question of faith, as I learned early, has to do with the hard side of life. Did God lead me into Maranatha? If so, why? If not, why did God let it happen to me? Those five years were undoubtedly the most difficult of my entire spiritual training, yet the transformation regarding my faith the most important. For years I concluded that no, God did not lead me there, that my own human side did, my own psychological need to control or have a perfect faith. I was barely nineteen, and I longed for boundaries and clarity. Blacks and whites. Fundamentalism offers clarity, then snatches it back.

I'd already spent my freshman and sophomore years living at college away from family. During my freshman year, I joined Alpha Phi Omega (APO), a service fraternity based on scouting principles, principles that were consistent with what was emerging as my own faith ethic. In APO, I met other boys, nee men, I came to respect, men who were in the process of teaching me normalcy and responsibility. Wouldn't continuing in APO have been a much less traumatic way to learn of the love of God? Besides, Maranatha was dysfunctional—an organization that acted like most maladjusted families, "bass-ackwards."

To ask again, did God lead me to join Maranatha, as I believed at the time? As though into some barren wilderness, to mold and shape me? Did God send the *Word* to test me? And if so, didn't I fail? By railing and shaking my fist at the very God I thought I was obeying?

I have no answer to these questions, even to this day, at least no adequate answer. Who can say whether God leads anyone through a wilderness from which that person will emerge scathed? Indeed, I have written previously that God, although not guiding me into storms, certainly knew ahead of time that I was headed into them and was never afraid for me. Never afraid for me to be tested, never afraid of the outcome. Faith is like that, and God is nothing if not faithful, as in *full of faith*.

I wonder whether we as a society approach modern education incorrectly. Everyone—parents, teachers, and students—treat tests as though they are the end, and not the means. Only they ought to be the means, oughtn't they? Isn't the goal of testing to help the teacher determine whether or not a student has learned what the teacher has tried to convey? And not to place a final assessment on a student, but to help the teacher know how to move forward with a student? A student that "fails" has not learned the lessons, meaning that it is time for the teacher to redouble his efforts. In other words, test results guide the teacher going forward.

Of course I can see the limitations to my thinking, and I am trained neither in education nor educational philosophy. My world is that of theology and faith, and this is the parallel: what if God tests us as a pedagogical tool, as a way to help us grow into spiritual maturity?

I have endured many struggles in my life: growing-up in an alcoholic family, straying from faith into legalism, struggling with identity and sexuality, losing a spouse to an impossibly painful disease, raising two children alone, enduring stalking as part of my job without institutional support, and facing headfirst a local church body that turned against me. Worst of all, I have had friends and family disown me. I would say that *none* of these wilderness experiences were ordained by God, but I would be quick to add that God was at my side through each struggle. The Divine Instructor used each era of my life to grow and mold me, to take me deeper, to love me more, and to teach me more of grace—always to teach me more of grace. I am a better person because I survived these trials, though I cannot imagine the God I know and love ordaining such awful times, testing or no testing. Yet, God pedagogically used each one, as the Book says, to refine me, loosen the dross, and purify the soul.

And so very importantly, God walked alongside me, inside of me, and around and with me as I journeyed. *I will never leave you nor forsake you.*

Who are you, O God? If not a patient and kind instructor of faith, molder of faith?

Thirty-Seven

ThanksGiving

THANKSGIVING.

I wasn't preaching that Sunday. Hugh Hardin was. Hugh was a retired priest who helped out at Christ Church in Sausalito so I could have a break from preaching once in a while. He also took the Christmas morning service so I could spend Christmas morning as a single parent with my two kids.

On that particular Sunday, I needed to drive Tate to Camp Noel Porter near Lake Tahoe for his week away. Summer, and the drive up and back could take anywhere from seven to eleven hours, depending on traffic. The day would be long, and I was so appreciative to Hugh for taking some of the load off of me.

I can't remember the particular Scripture readings, nor much of what he said. Sometimes a preacher makes a side comment, and that comment far more than the sermon sticks with you, or gets you thinking in a different way, which is what happened with me. I would have been in my late forties, and by now I'd struggled through parts of life in any number of ways—an alcoholic father, being in and leaving Maranatha (Christian cult), the death of a spouse, and like most other people, living through typical challenges. Yet, there I was, still alive. Still breathing. Still experiencing grace. And I amazed at this absolutely wonderful gift of life is.

Gift. Each breath I take is one more than I earned. Each breath is one more than I deserve. Each breath I take is something donated to me from somewhere else, free to me. Free to each of us, and at that awareness from whatever it was that Hugh said, I suddenly sensed something I'd only politely thought about before, gratitude. Spiritual gratitude.

So many Thanksgivings I've spent at a lovely and full dinner with family and friends when we circle the table trying to be *truly* thankful. "I'm thankful for my family." Or, "I'm thankful for my children." Or, "I'm grateful for a good job, and a good education." All important, and the ritual of giving thanks means practicing thanks, but seldom if ever on those Thanksgiving days did I experience much more than manufactured gratitude.

On that Sunday, though, and perhaps for the first time, I felt a deep and abiding gratitude. Spiritual gratitude, an awareness of the all in all that I've been given in a way that reached into the core of my being, my essence, my own *I am*, the God-part of me that is beyond me yet within me.

I've experienced that type of spiritual gratitude now over the years in different ways and seldom manufactured. It has sprung from somewhere deep inside, usually when my own self is set-aside and my taproot finds streams deep below, deep within.

I walked Camino de Santiago following my tough experience at and departure as rector from the Church of the Ascension (Knoxville, Tennessee). Walking Camino essentially means taking a pilgrimage walk across Spain, from France westward. I needed to clear my head and find out who I really am as a priest. Who I need to be. I cannot say it was a voice from above, but I walked away from Camino aware that I would not serve as rector again, that my time leading a parish in that role was over. As I contemplated that role, my role as priest, and my role as a father now of two adult children, I became—repeatedly, day after day—acutely grateful for my life as a priest. That though parts of it all had been arduous, stressful, and challenging—I nonetheless felt myself immeasurably fortunate to have been able to walk with people in a spiritual way, to pray for and with people, to have a career in which I could be daily devoted to a God of pure grace. I honestly cannot describe the deep awareness I had that so much of my priesthood—my humanity, if you will—was like each breath, gift upon gift upon gift. I deserved none of it, nobody does, but there it all was and is and is to come. Gift.

Aren't we the lucky ones?

Thirty-Eight

Creation and Salvation

JOHN O'DONAHUE TREATS STONE as one of his *Four Elements*. Writing of *stone,* he expresses gratitude at the removal of science from the concept of creation. In the beginning, he observes, was silence, and the silence was divided first by the whisper of word (my wording, not his), noting that the "projections of scientific intention" has been removed from our thoughts of creation, "unravel[ling] the false and smothering nets of language and thought which reduce creation to the false security of an interpreted world."[1]

"False security of an interpreted world," and perhaps you wonder, as do I, how to remove religion generally from the "false security of an interpreted world?" How might we experience faith rather than define it? If we do not first remove grace from words? Perhaps faith should not be reduced to creeds, doctrines and confessions, just as the name of God should not be spoken.

Although I am not a daily practitioner of centering prayer, I learned the principles of silence and contemplation from centering prayer. Although I am not a daily practitioner of the pentecostal speaking in tongues, I learned the principles of letting *spirit* express what mine and God's spirits need expressing (by opening my mouth without agenda).

1. O'Donohue, p. 127.

WHO AM I?

I find God in dirt, and through physical exertion, and by painting. I lose myself in each of these exercises in which words remain unformed, thoughts a sloppy mess rather than conjugated. Spirit communes with my spirit, and to borrow words from Jesus as written by John, I become One with the Son and One with the Father by the connection of the Holiest of Spirits.

It seems to me that centering prayer converges with contemplation, and contemplation with tongues, and tongues with dirt and dirt with exertion and exertion with painting. The objective of each these activities, or inactivities, being to lose myself, and intentionally or unintentionally to welcome a bit seed of grace. Congress among the Eternal and the temporal, between the Creator and the created. God loves me, touches me, and becomes *holy* within me.

CREATION AND SALVATION

> *Holy, Holy, Holy!*
> *Lord God Almighty*
> *All thy works shall praise thy name*
> *In earth and sky and sea*[2]

Never static, and indefinable using mere static terms, the Eternal is continuous movement, pouring and giving and spilling from one member of the Trinity each to the others, then from the godhead to you and to me and to all the earth. *For God so loved the world . . .*

We try so hard to understand God, but we tend to do so as a cerebral activity. Just as creation has been misunderstood as science, perhaps faith has been confused with doctrine, or vice versa, that doctrine has been confused with faith. What is the story of the garden anyway, if not marvelous mythology written to draw us into relationship? And what is doctrine anyway, but a pale mockery of faith?

The Creator still looks for us in the cool of the day: *for God so loved . . .* Far more than in sterile correct-thinking.

I love only because *Divine Love* first loved me. Found me in the cool of the day. And even my faith, my all, who I am and who I will become is and always was gift. I did not believe and become saved, I was saved and then believed. If any time element must be ascribed to the event at all. I never asked for faith, it was given to me.

One of my favorite concepts is that of being saved by faith, only Paul's letter to the Romans is ambiguous as to whose faith saves us. Mine? If so, that faith was gift. Jesus'? Even better, I am saved by someone else's faith, that of Jesus. Imagine that, and if these two are not so, that it is something I must do, then it is nothing more than work.

Even the term, *salvation,* carries heavy baggage. Are you saved? *Why no, and how unattractive of you to remind me.* Salvation is not about literal salvation from a fiery hell in the future; it is about salvation from a nihilistic existence in the present, from a

---

2. Reginald Heber, "Holy, Holy, Holy! Lord God Almighty," in *The Hymnal 1982* (New York: Church Publishing, 1985), no. 362.

life without meaning. I am saved with and for purpose, and if not to reach out as love to others, then for what?

When will we "unravel[ ] the false and smothering nets of language and thought which reduce" faith to the false security of an interpreted doctrine? When will we free Divine Mystery to be mysterious? When will we free God to be God?

Thirty-Nine

Who am I?

IF NOT A PRIEST?

A 94 year-old friend of mine, Meg, invited me to visit St. Michael's, her church on the upper west side of Manhattan. It was the Day of Pentecost. I forgot to wear red, though I did not forget, but chose not, to wear my clericals.

The first time I considered a call to the priesthood, I was a freshman in college, before Maranatha. Maybe what I felt was early call, a bare inkling to move in the direction of some magnetic pull. Like false labor pains. My bishop at the time told me that, were I to be called, he—they were all "he" in those days—would require me to work several years between college and seminary to get some real-world experience. I, of course, had no idea that it would take another twenty years before God would be ready for me.

I resisted that early false call primarily because I did not want to wear clericals. As I've explained, I prefer not to stand out. And, also as explained, I resist projections, particularly those of people I do not know.

Before church that Pentecost with Meg, I started thinking about myself, and what kind of priest that all makes me. Am *I ashamed of the Gospel*, to quote the Apostle? Of grace or of God? I don't think so, but returning to projections, I do not like people to assume a type of religiosity about me when they find out I am a priest. I am seldom the "religious" person people expect me to be.

Still, neither projections nor standing-out are the sum of it. I am not ashamed to be known as a priest at all; in fact, I am honored to be a priest. But I can be terribly un-priestly. And I do not like to have to explain myself to people. So what, then?

As the preacher spoke that morning, I started thinking about preaching, and call, and as she suggested to the congregation, making a *spiritual timeline*. That suggestion is why my spiritual timeline is included in this book, as it occurred to me that any reader would have a hard time following my chronology. Anyway, as I thought about my timeline, I remembered the catalyst to my *feeling* called to become a priest, and unlike many of my colleagues, I did not feel particularly called to perform the sacrament. Nor did I feel called to participate in the councils of the larger church, although that priestly duty is prescribed in my ordination vow. I was drawn for different reasons, some (to be honest) egotistical, to do each of these activities over the years. Yet, none of these are why I am a priest.

Rather, I felt called to share God's inescapable perfect and ubiquitous love with people who have experienced or heard only of a God who condemns, judges, causes bad things to happen, and hides from people. That is not the god I know. Not the god I experience.

The God I know is art and not science, is poetry and not history. The God I know is love and care and support and forgiveness and kindness and hope and grace. There is judgment, too, but not the judgment most people think of. God's is the educator's

WHO AM I?

judgment, the judgment of love, the love that patiently as a parent molds and moves us into better ways and directions.

I became a priest to share the love of *this* God, a love that, though often proclaimed, is under appreciated, accepted or lived.

I *preach* to share this love. I care for people *pastorally* to share this love. I *forgive* those who have wronged me to share this love. And I *write* to share this love.

Who am I? I am a lover of God and a free sharer of their love.

Abide in my love . . . Jesus invited.

> *Dance when you're*
> *broken open.*
> *Dance if you've*
> *torn the bandage off.*
> *Dance in the middle*
> *of the fighting.*
> *Dance in your blood.*
> *Dance when you're*
> *perfectly free.*
> —Rumi (Coleman Barks' edition)[1]

---

1. From *The Essential Rumi*, translated by Coleman Barks. ©1995 Coleman Barks. Used with acknowledgment under fair use.

Forty

Who are you, O God?

Love.
Ground of Being.
Elohim.
Sanctifier.
Divine Mystery.
Father.
El Shaddai.
Creator.
Instigator.
Mother.
Holy One.
Holy One of Israel.
Father.
Wisdom.
King.
Spirit.
Holy Spirit.
The Author of our Salvation.
The Faithful.
Daughter.
Lord.

www.ingramcontent.com/pod-product-compliance
Lightning Source LLC
Chambersburg PA
CBHW072137160426
43197CB00012B/2139

WHO ARE YOU, O GOD?

He/she who shall not be named.
Son.
YHWH.
Yahweh.
Judge.
Brother, Sister.
Wholly Other.
Ground of My Being.
I am.
I am what I am.
I will be what I will be.
Unnamed.
Indefinable.

Wind.
Love.